PRAISE FOR ARE YOU A MANAGER OR A LEADER?

"With the title of this book, Scott Comey asks an important question on which we should all reflect. Throughout, he draws on a depth of experience, personal stories, historical perspective, popular culture, bright minds, and interactive steps. In person and in video, you can lead more effectively with this guidance."

— **Ethan Beute**, Chief Evangelists a BombBomb, coauthor of *Rehumanize Your Business*, and host of *The Customer Experience Podcast*

"Scott Comey's Are You a Manager or a Leader? is a masterful blueprint for successful leadership. With a mix of high-level concepts and street-level tactics, Scott gives you everything you need to become the leader you want to be. From building trust to defining your mission to knowing your numbers, Scott explains both the why and the how of essential leadership skills. Want to lead, or lead more effectively? Then read this book—and you're well on your way."

— **Adam Contos**, CEO, RE/MAX Holdings, Inc.

"I really enjoyed Scott Comey's book on leadership especially his delivery of key themes through personal stories. They were gripping, impactful, and memorable and made us want to read more. Scott's focus on "self" and how we are always going to be the more powerful effecting change in ourselves instead of blaming others, is a message so needed today for the world's leaders. If you are a business leader and have others looking to you for direction, this is a must-read."

– Tyrone K. Davids,
CPA MBA & CEO of EDI Performance

"This book is needed more than ever. We still have far too many managers and not enough leaders. Scott lays out a compelling case and powerful benefits that SOLID leadership provides. He's worked through adversity multiple times and the growth of his team is proof of his expertise. Get this book. Read and apply its wisdom, especially during these turbulent times."

– Tony Rubleski, Bestselling Author, Mind Capture book series

ARE YOU A
MANAGER
OR A
LEADER?

How to Inspire Results Through Others

SCOTT COMEY

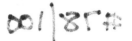

Design & Distribution by Bublish, Inc.

ISBN: 978-1-64704-322-3 (eBook)
ISBN: 978-1-64704-323-0 (Paperback)
ISBN: 978-1-64704-324-7 (Hardcover)

This book is dedicated to my beloved Uncle Fritz Heaton. My Uncle Fritz unfortunately won't have an opportunity to see this first book of mine, but I know that he would be extremely proud. As a writer for the Western Journal of Medicine, he inspired me to follow my passion for writing. A passion I started years ago in High School when my Uncle was still with us. He has since passed. I think about him often. Thank you, Uncle Fritz. I love you and miss you.

CONTENTS

Introduction IX

Chapter 1: Leaders Tell the Truth 1
Chapter 2: Leadership versus Management 5
Chapter 3: Turn the Dial in your Life and Business 15
Chapter 4: Building Trust and Loyalty with Your Team ... 21
Chapter 5: Look in the Mirror 29
Chapter 6: Identifying Opportunity 37
Chapter 7: Leaders Seek to Grow Personally 43
Chapter 8: Never Be Content & Know your Numbers 47
Chapter 9: Leading Through Challenging Times 55
Chapter 10: Leading Through Video 69
Chapter 11: Leaders Reflect & Show Care 77
Chapter 12: Leaders Give 89
Chapter 13: Leading with FUN 95
Chapter 14: Leaders Create Value 99

Conclusion 103
A Word on Training 105
Acknowledgement 113
About the Author 115

INTRODUCTION

E very day we are faced with challenges in our workplace. Some challenges brought on by consumers; some brought on by our employees; some challenges that we create for ourselves. Management is such a broad category, but in general it can be summed up to bringing a group of individuals together in order to accomplish a goal using resources provided. As a manager, it is our job to oversee the process and the people per guidelines given to us, or in some cases, created by us.

Some of the best companies have developed exceptional leaders over time. Leaders that have come up from the ranks of "management." So what is a Leader? How do they differ from a Manager? Is there a difference? Absolutely.

Over the course of my life I have been both a manager and a leader. This book is intended to help transform the person who may currently be managing, into an incredible leader that drives even better results and creates a powerful culture that attracts more consumers and other great employees. Before we dive in, I think it's important that you get to know where my journey started.

I have navigated my way throughout my professional life, trying to discover how to be a better leader. It has never been easy and still isn't today. I started my professional career in management approximately 27 years ago by becoming the acting Store Manager for Burger King in my hometown of Big Bear, CA at the ripe age of 17. After high school I ended up joining the military reserves, first serving in the US Army and then re-enlisted into the Air Force. At the end of my time in the military reserves I had become a Non-Commissioned Officer, a Staff Sergeant. The Air Force also helped mold me by sending me to Leadership Schools where I started to change my experience from "Management" to "Leadership". What is the difference between the two you might ask? Management is simply managing people, managing projects, managing something. And this is in no way to diminish management. I loved being a manager. I got very good at managing people and businesses.

But when defining leadership it is slightly different in that it is the act of getting people, employees, soldiers etc. to follow the direction you lay out for them. Good leaders can get their people to do amazing things because they want to and not because they have to. They see a clear picture of what their actions can provide, or what the end result can be, because the example has been laid out in a vision by their leader. The leader has painted a great picture of what success looks like. Success of a project, of a business, of winning a battle.

After spending many years as a non-commissioned officer in the military reserves, and many years in management, I decided to start a real estate brokerage. In fact, I decided to start a real estate brokerage in 2008. Not that anyone needs a reminder as to what 2008 brought our economy in the US, but the housing market crashed, and the economy took a deep dive into the Great Recession. Yes, this was when I thought it would be good to open a real estate brokerage.

Let me give some context as to the "WHY." I was at a regional real estate brokerage at the time, and just selling, not an owner. The economy started to crash, people were losing their jobs, and home sales declined rapidly. This meant my income declined rapidly as did almost everyone else in my field of work. The owners of the company I was at almost immediately reacted by taking away. Taking away office space, as in cutting our square footage in the office in half. Taking away tools and resources that they used to pay for to help us in our business. It was like kicking us while we were down. It wasn't bad enough that we were having a hard enough time getting homes sold and actually making money, but now we were also having to dig into our small pocketbooks to pay for marketing and other tools that used to be part of what was included by belonging to this brokerage. There was a strong feeling that the ownership of that office was not managing the situation well. Their vision was reactive. There was clearly no plan for a scenario like this and it was not jiving well within the office.

There were no meetings to discuss a game plan for what to do in the coming economy. There were no ideas given to us in regard to alternative ways to make money in our industry in the changing times. What would you do if this situation were presented to you? Would you lose confidence in the ownership? Would it inspire you to maybe start your own real estate company?

It was in August of 2008 that I founded Real Estate Bundle LLC. The vision was to be an independent brokerage with the sole purpose of providing relevant, reasonable support to agents during a down market. My concept of the "bundle" was to offer different levels of service to sellers, and the company, my company, would pay for some of the marketing of the listings. Something that wasn't really being done by anyone at the time. Especially in this down economy. That is what I believed a leader should do. Step up and provide in times of despair.

It was not easy. In fact, the real estate market lost about half of the agent base between 2008—2011. Another 25% or so went and got part-time jobs doing something to try and supplement their incomes. We saw many other competitors go out of business. Offices around us started to close.

Life was not easy for me either. We moved our office 3 times in three years to make sure we always had a location that we could afford. I did what I had to do, to provide for my agents and still pay for some of their marketing. I was able to recruit a few agents over and even trained a couple of brand-new agents during this time. I did research on what my company should be doing to be proactive in this changing market. My agents got Distressed Property designations and education, and we got really good at handling short sales on properties. Short sales became our bread and butter for a while. It was a tough time to watch my friends lose their homes to foreclosure and short sales. But leaders won't go into the fetal position during times like this. They find the vision that will carry their people through any storm and they garner the confidence to move forward believing that there is light at the end of the tunnel. I also believe a true quality of a leader is someone who can remain calm in choppy waters. When everything seems to be going to the garbage around you the last thing you want is for your people to see the stress on you. Therefore, I love the analogy of the flight attendant in rough turbulence on a plane. Can you imagine if they freaked out every time the plane shook? The passengers would scream and be nervous. We need to be the flight attendants in our business. Our business is our plane. As long as we put the mask on ourselves first and know where the emergency exits are (should we need them), then we will make it from point A to point B with little stress.

Let's stay on this analogy of the flight attendant. When they go up and down the aisles on the plane offering snacks and beverages, this helps build trust and puts you at ease. So, in the event of an emergency, they become a trusted leader.

In 2008–2011, I felt like a flight attendant on a plane in rough turbulence. I was afraid, I had to borrow money, I had to move my office multiple times. I even got a part-time job delivering wine to be able to afford our lease, but we landed that plane without losing any passengers.

In 2011, as the economy started to come out of the recession, I realized that I wanted more for my agents. More than a small independent broker can offer them. The agents deserved better tools, better websites, better resources, and honestly a better brand. So, I explored a few options of franchises and decided to partner with RE/MAX in 2012. Why RE/MAX? They had a great vision. They had amazing leadership. And as stated already, that is what's needed for success in any business. Great Leadership.

So now that you have a brief backstory on me. You may be asking, why this book? So often in society we are patted on the back for not doing much. We are told "Great job" when maybe it was mediocre. We are handed trophies for participation. We've watched this in our society occasionally lead to less than exceptional kids, less than exceptional workers, and less than exceptional businesses. I have become a study of people and my peers. What do the successful people in business consistently do? What do they avoid? In a real estate brokerage, you are running a business with several smaller businesses under you (Independent Contractors). It is a tough business to run successfully. After over a decade now of owning a real estate brokerage with four locations, and two mortgage office locations, it was time to share what's been learned along the way about transforming from management to a leader.

Not only will you hear my personal stories and observations, but also the stories and observations of many others who have witnessed greatness behind their own doors. The common threads of becoming a great leader.

By the end of this book, my goal is that it will inspire you to look at your role within your organization differently. Inspire you to change how you look at your staff. Get you thinking from a different perspective.

With decades of leadership experience myself, most recently as a Mega 1000 Broker Owner in real estate, my hope is that you will have faith in the information that is shared in this book. The good, the bad, the ugly, will all be shared. Hang on and garner what you need in your business today to move forward towards a better business and to become a leader.

Whether you are an entry level manager at your company, an Executive within a corporation, run a small team or own your own business, we hope you garnish some golden nuggets that will help you become the leader you are destined to be.

CHAPTER 1

Leaders Tell the Truth

What would come of a military battle if the leader told his soldiers only what they wanted to hear? What if he lied? Could the battle be won? I can tell you that if you read every speech that has been published about war heroes and the leaders that led their troops, led their soldiers into harm's way, they always told the truth. Why? Because that is what is needed to succeed or to have the chance of succeeding.

I was recently watching the movie Midway, about the battle at Midway just after the attack on Pearl Harbor. In one scene in the movie, the Colonel says "Boys, we are getting ready to head into harm's way. We will be vastly outnumbered, and most of you won't make it back."

As I envision myself in the shoes of the pilots I am wondering what is going on in their minds. They are basically being told that 2 out of 3 of them are going to die. Why is this important to tell the pilots? Why not just lie and say, "We have the upper hand. We plan to win this, now let's go boys."

I can tell you what the difference is for me. It is the fact that when I am told the truth, I trust my leader. I trust when they say "Let's go over here." I trust when they say "Let's not go over there." Versus the commanding officer that lies and you end up seeing most of your buddies die. What's the likelihood you would follow him into battle again? Slim to none. I believe that when a leader tells the truth it creates a scenario where a person might be better at their job than if lied to. For example, if you told me I have a good chance of coming home alive and this would be an easy battle, I might not be so aware when out in the field. I may not prepare as much as I might if I knew that I likely wouldn't come back, because you gave me confidence that the level of survival is high.

If the commander instead stated that most of you won't be coming home and we will be massively outnumbered, well now I know I need to be alert and at my best in order to survive.

You see the difference?

It's like the coach that tells his team this will be an easy game. Have you ever been watching your team play a game against a weak opponent and said "This is going to be a blow out!"? I know that I sometimes don't even watch the game because it may be boring or slow.

I remember one time coaching a pee wee football team and we were #1 in our area and league. We were getting ready to face the worst team in our league. They had never even won a single game. We went in as leaders and coaches knowing this. We even verbalized this to our young players. When the game came, we ran up the score early on as we knew we would. But then, we got too comfortable. We started trying plays we have always wanted to try but never had the guts to try them in a real game. We ventured outside the game plan and the players followed our lead because they trusted this "new" plan would work.

None of them did and we ended up turning over the ball. Then the other team started playing very well. It was strange. We could not believe what was happening. Our scoring lead dwindled and before we knew it, this team was poised to win the game and in fact they did.

So, what was the lesson here? Same as I shared above. Our head coach and the rest of us coaches decided to rotate in different personnel, run trick plays, and just plain have fun because "Of course we are going to crush this team." The other coaches likely told the truth, and their players heard them loud and clear. I have always wondered what those coaches said to their players before the game. I imagine it went something like this, "Ok guys. We are getting ready to play the top team in the league. They have never lost a game. They are bigger than us and they are better than us. BUT, we have a chance if we just play our best and execute the fundamentals that we teach in practice."

On my team, our players knew that our opponent that day was bad. Our ego as leaders got the best of us and we did not prepare our team the way we should have. We played very good in the first half of the game, but a great leader knows that there is a clock in everything we do. In the 2nd half we played horribly. I'm sure the other team was very much aware that it would be even harder than all of their other opponents to pull off a victory. But they played their best, we did not, and they won.

You see, if faced with overwhelming odds that you are made aware of, I believe you can overcome anything. That team overcame a huge challenge, beating our top performing team. My team lost because we got comfortable. Nothing great is achieved in the "comfort zone." We assumed the game was in the bag. The players just didn't play to their best.

Walter Lord once said, "Even against the greatest of odds, there is something in the human spirit—a magic blend of skill, faith and valor—that can lift men from certain defeat to incredible victory."

In his masterpiece bestselling book Man's Search for Meaning, Viktor Frankl shares a concept of "provisional existence." In referencing concentration camps he speaks of how a person has a hard time living for the future when there is no end in sight for their "prison term." This was so powerful for me to hear when I read this. For one, I can't even

3

imagine being in those incredibly difficult circumstances. On the other hand, I understood this concept of finding a reason to live. There is a famous quote by Friedrich Nietzsche that says "He who has a why to live, can bear almost any how." For my little pee wee football example above, that team we played had a strong why. They wanted to win their first game, and who says it can't be against the best team in the league?

Leaders know how to be honest and how to get their folks to understand their own WHY, or the WHY of the greater good. For the Midway pilots, their WHY was revenge. The leaders definitely found ways to incorporate this as well into their strategy to win that battle. But first and foremost, be honest. Don't lie. Your people deserve to hear the truth. They will follow you if you remain honest with them in every scenario, regardless of how grim sometimes the outcome looks.

CHAPTER 2

Leadership versus Management

I have often wondered what the big differences are in being a leader versus being a manager. I feel like I have a good understanding of these differences, only because I have been both at different times in my career. But without firsthand knowledge or experience, how can we describe the differences?

I reached out to several folks that I trust that I believe are great leaders in their respective industries and companies. I wanted to see if I found common threads between the thought process of these folks. Many of the individuals I interviewed are Executives at companies in industries ranging from Financial Management, to Real Estate, to Executive Coaching and Training companies.

I've already shared some thoughts on being a leader VS. A manager, but let's take a deeper dive.

LEADERSHIP

Inspiration: Leaders tend to be inspiring folks. Or they are always trying to find ways to inspire others. To find the positive in every situation. Can you imagine a scenario where the sky was falling, and you shared with your group this fact without hope or direction? Devastation would kick in and it could lead to the sky falling even quicker. I believe you can be honest while being inspiring. It's all in how you state things to your people. Things will get bad at times. You may be up against overwhelming odds, but just like the Pee Wee football team that beat my team way back in the day, your word choice and demeaner can change the outcome of the game.

I have a current leader in my company who often says, "Don't be jealous, be inspired." Inspiration lifts you up. When you are jealous it brings you down. Think about it. If someone "inspires" you instead, it's as if to say, I love what they are all about and one day I too will be that way. It quickly eliminates the jealously.

Be a Good Listener: Empathy is such an amazing strength. Do you think empathy is something you can improve in? I believe you absolutely can. Being willing to take time for your people. To listen. Not just to concerns about work, but actual caring about them and their families. After all, by helping your people be better at work, you are affecting their home life and families as well. If your people are happy at work, that should translate into a healthier home life. Leaders tend to inspire us to be better versions of ourselves.

Sacrifice: What would it mean if a leader was to sacrifice? After several interviews, this was definitely a character trait that made the top of the list. Leaders do sacrifice at times for the greater good. There are so many things I can share in this segment. (about this trait?) Where do I start? First, there is the sacrifice of time. Leaders typically tend to work longer hours than their people. Not just because they often aren't hourly employees, but because they know that the extra time, the extra effort, will result in a better place or better results for the overall company and its workforce. Time is probably the biggest sacrifice. I know many of the leaders I interviewed are parents, some of very young children who also rely on them. Yet leaders will sacrifice, or at a minimum have to balance family life and work life.

I know my wife Renée and I realize how much we've sacrificed for the greater good of our company. For example, we have reinvested almost every dollar we made as high producing sales individuals to grow the company and to be able to provide better tools that would help our agents sell more homes. Leaders also will sacrifice profits for the community. Almost every leader I talked to goes through great expense of company funds to host events that raise money or awareness for various worthy organizations in their communities. Renée and I have done this for years. Obviously this takes from OUR pockets, BUT we also realize, and I think most leaders do, that we wouldn't be where we are today without the support of the communities that we serve. Could I have more money today if we didn't sacrifice profits to growing the company and giving back? Absolutely. However, I believe leaders don't lead to become rich. Leaders lead because they want to leave a lasting impact. That is our goal always. We want to leave our communities better than we found them. We want to leave our agents and staff setup for future growth and success for them and their families.

Zig Ziglar is famously known for saying, "You can have everything in life you want, if you just help enough people get what they want." I not only believe this, but it is becoming true. One of the things I want in life is to see others accomplish their life aspirations and I have seen this already several times over. I've seen several people get out of debt, join Country Clubs, pay cash for wedding rings and much more. This makes my heart melt. If I have had any impact on helping these folks achieve these things, by me myself doing what I can to help them, then I am already successful. I think leaders think this way, where Managers, maybe not so much.

Personal Growth: I would venture to say that there are a variety of leaders If there was a leadership chart, I believe that the GREAT leaders (the ones that would be considered at the top of this chart), are lifelong learners. This came up multiple times in my interviews. Great leaders believe that they don't know it all and are always of the understanding that they can grow further.

I personally had not been a reader. In fact, I've often shared how from the time I was born until about age 38 I read maybe a total of 15 books in my life. Most fictional. Something changed in me as our company started to grow. I kept going to conferences where the speaker would recommend a book. So, I'd buy the book. I wouldn't read it though. My wife would. Then she would speak about how amazing the content was and all that she learned from the book. It dawned on me that I might be missing out. No matter how much I hated reading at the time, and honestly struggled to focus, I started forcing myself to read. Just a few pages at a time. That eventually turned into 10 pages a day, and eventually I started to learn and learn and learn some more. In fact, about 5 years ago I had an epiphany that some of these business books took decades for the author to write. Super successful business icons have garnered all they learned in their 10, 20, 30+ years into a couple hundred-page book. If you read their book, you would fast forward your success and not take 10, 20 or 30 years like they did to get there. This book even is a culmination of almost 30 years of my personal experience from managing and leading in varying industries and various companies, which hopefully shortens your path in the transition from manager to leader.

People have lived before you. Don't reinvent the wheel. The blueprint to success is not in shiny object syndrome, but in a book. Find it, read it, and take action on what you learn.

So why wouldn't I read? I now am a massive reader and absolutely love it. I have learned so much. I am constantly sharing with my audiences that I am a student of others that have lived before me.

I am not self-made. I am a product of Darren Hardy, Brian Buffini, Brian Tracy, Zig Ziglar, Jim Rohn, Brian Moran and so many others that have fast tracked me to a path that I love.

Focus: Great leaders find within themselves to focus so that they get shit done. My wife is WAY better than me at being a GSD person, but I am a student and constantly trying to get better. I have for years embraced the concept of not reinventing the wheel. This is a Mantra of mine. So often I see salespeople and entrepreneurs trying to find that quick path to success. That shiny object that will get them the instant success. You know what I believe creates success? A clear and focused, proactive approach to constantly learning and improving yourself. As I am writing this book right now I am in a hotel lobby in South Boston and reflecting on a speaking engagement I was at yesterday that had almost 800 people. The Corona Virus had become enough of a concern as people became aware of it that it caused many attendees to switch to a virtual version, yet almost 800 people attended in person. I stepped on stage and it was the first thing I addressed. The emotional guy I am, I teared up for a moment looking out into a sea of real estate agents eager to learn and ready to take great notes. Personal growth. Along with those watching from home, they came to invest in themselves. You know who didn't register? The real estate agents that are trying to find the quick path to wealth. You want to know what leaders have embraced? The quickest way to wealth and success is a constant and never-ending desire to grow by learning from those that have lived before you. Tony Robbins in his book "Personal Power" coined the acronym CANI. "Constant and Never-ending Improvement."

While we are on the topic, I remember watching a documentary on Warren Buffet where they mentioned that Bill Gates' mom invited Warren Buffet over for dinner with Bill Gates, and the story goes that she asked both Bill and Warren to write down one word which has helped cause their success over the years. They both wrote down the same word, "FOCUS."

For me, I have found time blocking to be the best way to help myself focus. I have learned though that we all have different ways to focus. Some folks just cannot embrace the time blocking idea. I personally love it. I can stay in a "block" and not get distracted. I don't want to spend too much time here on time blocking, because it may truly not be for everyone, but if you struggle to focus, I encourage you to find books on the topic to improve that aspect of yourself.

Final thoughts on leadership:

Leaders tend to be remembered in history. Why? Because they tend to put others needs first. If you think about historic people that have impacted our world, John F Kennedy, Martin Luther King and others. It is because of their proactive desire to help others. To make policy or create change that was sometimes not popular. To get results or an outcome that vastly impacted others, not themselves. If you think about Presidents that tried to just do something to make a name for themselves while in office, they aren't memorable, right? They aren't in the history books. Unless their selfish acts ended up becoming publicly known and trials took place. Then those Presidents went down in history, but in a negative way. Leaders are selfless.

Taking out the trash. Someone has to do it. Managers know that there is a specific person who has that job and they tend to just make sure that person does it. Leaders might just take out the trash themselves. They lead by example. Personally, I would never ask an employee of mine to do anything I wouldn't do myself. Roll up your sleeves and do some dishes. Clean a toilet on occasion. But do it because it's not below you. Not to make a point.

MANAGERS

For a good chunk of my career, I was a manager. Now that I've been a leader, I definitely see the main differences. Let me start out by giving you the definition of a Manager. A manager is someone who is responsible for controlling or administering all of part of a company. For example, I was once a Store Manager for a coffee shop, bookstore, and shoe store. In every role, my duties included:

- TO create and manage a schedule for all staff
- Uphold company policies
- Execute performance reviews and disciplinary action or plans for staff
- Manage expenses and control costs
- Manage inventory and control theft and loss
- Manage the customer experience, including company expectations for greeting, upselling and store cleanliness

I did all of these things great. I was a great manager in my day. I also managed some other great managers who were my Assistants over the years. I trained them to also become great managers to the point where many of my managers went on to become Store Managers themselves. I took great pride in this. Other managers would ask, aren't you upset you are constantly losing great managers to run other locations? I would say, "No, because that is fulfilling to me." I think this feat started me down a path of wanting to do more. I liked the feeling of helping impact someone else's life. It wasn't long before I took on additional roles and duties and even switched careers to eventually become a leader.

So how do I sum up Managers versus Leaders? Directing versus Inspiring? I don't want to make it sound like Managers can't also be great leaders within their organization. In fact, in every retail environment there are great Store Managers, that also are great leaders. They have become leaders to their team and to their peers. It is possible to be both a great Manager and a great Leader. To me, Leaders are impacting others, not just placating a company to get a promotion or raise. Leaders are selfless and give their time. They invest time to help others. With Managers it is sometimes very difficult to give too much time to help others, only because the workload put on you does not allow a lot of extra time to develop and work on helping others.

When asking one of my current peers what her perception of the difference is between Leaders and Managers, she shared "…management is more about enforcing rules and keeping people in line." I know that sounds harsh, but I have to agree, to a certain degree, with this statement. Managers are put in place to not question the rules, but to enforce them. Leaders are typically part of creating the rules, but then they hire managers to help enforce. It's just a necessary part of the company model. Leaders tend to be visionaries looking forward and cannot be crippled with the day to day enforcement or handling of challenges that come up.

In asking another great leader I know about his take on what is a manager, he responded with "…Management drives action through compelled compliance." I summarize it like this, Leaders create the game plan for the year, for the next few years, then inspire managers to help achieve the goals. Managers are given benchmarks that they can work directly side by side with direct reports to ensure those benchmarks are hit.

It takes all of the moving pieces for a successful company to thrive. Great leadership to set clear expectations and great management to work on achieving these goals. In asking my business coach about leaders versus managers, Tyrone Davids with EDI replied, "Leaders are the designers of the organization and set the vision and direction for the company, while Managers are the doers that take the vision and implement with the resources given."

Tyrone further explained that both leaders and managers lead by example and "have a high level of integrity and authenticity." To be good at either, he also mentions that they must be great communicators and have the ability to motivate.

I also believe that another common trait of both Leaders and Managers is the ability to Trust. No one likes a Micro-manager, so we need to know that it is ok to not hover over our employees. They will be more likely to perform and execute your tasks if given the trust to accomplish it.

CHAPTER 3

Turn the Dial in your Life and Business

I t was the Fall of 2012 when my real estate brokerage started to grow at a quick pace. We were recovering quickly out of The Great Recession, and I was still selling real estate back then. I needed help. My wife Renee was at the time running one of the largest KOHL's Department stores in the country and was extremely successful in the company. And even though the income she brought home was particularly good, I truly needed her to quit and come help at our company. It wasn't an easy decision because we then would be "all in" within our company. It was risky and now all our eggs are in one basket.

This gives me a great chance to share why being "all in" and cutting your lifeline is an important part of moving towards success in business. I stated earlier that owning a real estate brokerage has given me a unique opportunity to see several agents grow an extremely profitable business, and many others never get going, waste money, kill their savings, and have to quit real estate and go back to a W2 job. Well, one of the biggest reasons is that they still had a lifeline of a full-time or part-time job outside of being a Real Estate agent. This security made it to where the financial pressure wasn't enough to warrant going through the pain of actually properly owning a business. The folks that tried to start their real estate business while working another job, tended to stay in their comfort zone. Success rarely comes to those who stay in their comfort zone.

Back to my wife. We were all in. We had to make her leaving KOHLS work for us. It reminds me of the story of the Spanish Commander Hernan Cortez in 1519 AD during the conquest of Mexico. Hernan arrived at the battle amongst many ships and ordered that his own ships get burned before heading in to battle. Essentially telling his people that we aren't leaving here in retreat. We win or we die. Those are the options. When you lose the lifeline, you fight harder. And as a leader, you fight harder for yourself, to power through the tough times and move towards the direction of success.

Well with us, it worked. Renee got her license and quickly was enthralled in our brokerage, and we continued to grow and thrive. Over the years, as we coached our own agents in their businesses, we started to understand the concept of making little changes today that would lead to great success later in life.

One of my favorite books is the Compound Effect by Darren Hardy. Essentially that is what this book showcases. How if you make little, subtle changes today, that may even seem insignificant, it will transform your life later. The reason is that these little changes you make get compounded as the years go by. There is a ripple effect. I always paint this picture in my own mind as to a pot of water on the stove that you are trying to boil. If you turn the burner knob ever so slightly, let's say to the first notch, the water starts to get just a bit warmer. It's no longer cold water. Now turn the burner knob one more notch, and the water gets even warmer. One more notch, even warmer, and eventually you turn the knob enough notches up on the dial and the water will boil.

This is what we have seen over the years in people's businesses. Not just real estate, but several other businesses that we've analyzed over decades. It doesn't take some life changing thing today, as much as it is small positive changes over time that will cause a ripple effect on your business.

Several years after Renee joined the Real Estate firm and well after we "burned our ships", we started a Podcast to share our tidbits, or as I like to call them, "nuggets," with business owners. We decided to name our podcast "Turn the Dial." In the spirit of the burner knob analogy I gave above, as you read through the following chapters, try to find areas that you can just start to make small changes in your business or in your management style. Whether you are a business owner, a manager, or an Executive we look to help share some golden nuggets for you.

You have to grab the knob before you can turn the dial. So as leaders we need to identify what knob to grab. For some of us it is in the area of growing our customer base. What are some things we know that if we did them, it would result in more customers? As a brokerage owner, my customer is the real estate agents that work at our firm. If you are a team leader or real estate agent, your customer is the consumer looking to buy or sell a home.

Make a list of all of those things that can help you attract more customers. After you have a pretty good-sized list, narrow it down to your top few things that when implemented would have the greatest result on increasing customers. In the New York Times bestselling book, the 12 Week Year, Brian Moran and Michael Lennington call this "mind mapping." Picture creating a funnel where every good idea to grow your business can be put in at the top, but we don't always have time or capacity to do them all. Moran & Lennington encourage you to focus on the few things that would have the biggest impact in that area of your business. Now in some cases it may be uncomfortable to do what you know will have the biggest impact. That's why we call it

Turn the Dial. Grab the knob. In time we can start to turn the knob. Before you know it, your business will be boiling.

I'd love to paint this picture just a bit clearer with an actual example. In a sales business, one of the best ways to grow your business or get referrals is by making calls. Whether they be cold calls or calls to a database of people you know. Some of the top agents I know in real estate make 15, 20, 30 calls a week. Week after week, and they get tons of referrals to consumers who need to buy or sell their home. Call reluctance is one of the biggest hurdles that stops and paralyzes some agents from even making the calls. When we coach real estate agents, we recommend that those agents start by making just one call a day. Now that may seem like way too low, but I promise you it is not. That is my version of just "grabbing the knob." Over the next several months, we end up getting them to go from one a day to several per day. They start to get used to habit of picking up the phone. They get used to the habit of making time for the calls. And eventually, they get used to tough conversations they sometimes have while on a call. I've shared so many examples like this over our years of coaching high performers, and several started out just like this. One call per day. Over time, they get to 10 calls per week, then 20, 30 and on. This is why we call it, Turn the Dial. Your business is like a pot of water, and if we need to get to boiling, let's just start you at filling the pot with water, and grabbing the knob.

As leaders we must understand this concept. We must know that for ourselves, we can utilize this concept to drastically transform our company's current circumstances, by just choosing today to start. Over time, that compound effect in our business will happen. As leaders, it is our responsibility to get our employees, our agents, our team to trust this form of thinking as well. I know we live in a world of instant gratification, but almost every business book you can read will tell the story of slow and steady wins the race. Or, the tortoise always wins, not the hare. Or, Patience is one of the most powerful virtues of a leader because greatness takes time. If we fully understand this concept ourselves, then we should be able to help our people understand it and greatness will come. Albert Einstein is famously known for saying that "Compound Interest is the 8th wonder of the world. He who understands it, earns it. He who doesn't, pays it." In this, he is not sharing a way to get rich quick. He is stating that there is a method to growth, that if you know and trust the path, you can have those riches over time, as your action, the deposits you make, will lead to wealth after being compounded over time. Albert Einstein is also famous for saying "Insanity: Doing the same thing over and over again and expecting a different result." The beauty of turning the dial, is that by making small incremental changes in your business, you are absolutely doing something different. Over time, that difference will lead to success, not insanity.

Continue to make it a priority as a leader to remind your team that success does not happen overnight. Be patient, do what you know will lead you in the right direction, and then have faith that the results will come.

I am often reminded that people have lived before me. One of the main reasons I love to read is it allows me to quickly garner the knowledge of the author. In many cases, it took the author decades to get enough knowledge to even put together a book, to share it to the world so that we can learn what to do and what not to do, quicker than if the reader learned it themselves. Your staff need to learn from you so that they save time as well. Having faith is about believing that if someone has done X, Y and Z and achieved success, then you too should be able to do X, Y and Z and expect similar success. The challenge comes when we do not see the results quick enough. So, having faith is extremely important. In the book Think and Grow Rich, Napoleon Hill shares how "Faith" is the second step to riches. He states that "Life's battles don't always go to the stronger or faster man, but...the one who wins is the one who thinks he can." You must believe that what you are doing will result in your desired outcome. People have lived before you. It will work for you too. The challenge becomes, when? We all know that we have control over the activities, but not always the results from those activities. Focus on DOING the activities. It does not matter how small you start, just start. And then have faith. Don't lose faith. Trust that your results too will come, and they will.

I'd love to tell one more story about "Turning the Dial" as it pertains to health. I remember just 9 months ago telling my wife that I am sick of being overweight. I do not like the way I look and I am finally ready to do something about it. Problem was I did not do much exercise back then. It was challenging for me to even think about running or doing any exertion of exercise. So, she encouraged me to just go for a walk each day for one mile. Now back then I thought, what is walking going to do? And one mile is a joke. Little did I realize that she was "turning the dial" on me. After a month straight of that I felt good enough to turn the dial up to walking a mile and a half each day. As my body got used to this new habit and as my muscles started to develop on these walks, I eventually got to running a mile each day. Then a month later, running a mile and half each day, then two miles a day. Then on to 2.25 miles a day for 30 days straight, and now I am up to a minimum of 2.5 miles that I run, not walk. 9 months of this compound effect and I am 25 pounds lighter and the healthiest I've been in almost 13 years. As I started moving more, faster and for longer distances, I noticed my body craving different foods. Now I am eating foods that my body actually needs. Food that I never thought I would even crave. Over time, small adjustments have led me to a healthier life. So, what are YOU going to do to Turn the Dial in your business, in your health? Grab the knob and decide today that you are going to move towards making incremental positive changes as a leader that will get your brokerage / team / business further along towards your goals.

CHAPTER 4

Building Trust and Loyalty with Your Team

"I've learned years ago that it is way more important to be respected by your people than liked."

One of the best ways to become an incredible leader is to garner the trust and loyalty of your staff or salespeople. The big question though is, how do you do this? How do you even measure something like trust? How do you know if your employees are happy? How do you know if you are providing the right tools, resources, benefits?

I have so many things that can be shared on this topic. I will start though by talking about one of the best ways that I did it, which was using third party surveys.

Surveymonkey.com has been for years now my favorite place to go to create surveys to analyze where we are as a company. It is a relatively inexpensive way to conduct surveys without formally hiring much more expensive independent researchers to get the same information.

Surveymonkey.com also has a way for you to allow the surveys you create and send out to be anonymous which will get more candid responses to your questions.

On average, I sent these surveys out about once every 18 months or so. Here are some examples for you to use:

For leaders, I would ask questions like:

1. What is the most enjoyable part of your job?
2. How do you prefer to be recognized for a job well done? (Higher pay, bonuses, awards, promotion to a higher-level job)
3. If there is one thing you could change about our company, what would it be?

For salespeople, I would ask questions like:

1. What is your biggest challenge right now in the business?
2. If you can think of one tool or resource that we should have, what would it be?
3. Is there anything that the company currently provides that you don't take advantage of, or think might be a waste of company money?

We even created a survey once that revolved around getting feedback on staff and leadership. We asked specific questions to help us analyze how everyone viewed folks in our real estate brokerage, but specifically the leaders.

Using surveys, like surveymonkey.com, will allow you to improve aspects of your company for the better. Doing something with the information you learn by going through an exercise like this will garner trust from your people. They want to be at a company that is always looking to be better. I think the first step in doing this is to ask what's broken and what's working.

This is a very humbling experience because surveyed individuals will provide honest and sometimes very raw truth. You need this truth because we don't want to waste money on tools they aren't using, and we don't want them to leave our company and move their license to another brokerage over something minor we could've changed in the company, had we just asked the right questions. Is there something small that you are doing that might be causing stress to your staff? This process can allow you to find out before it causes damage to your team.

The next step is to take the broken items and work on improving or removing them from your company. On the things that are working, you may need to expand on those, since they are favored company wide.

Another thing I love about surveymonkey.com is that the participants don't have to see the results. The reason that this is important, is that the participants in the survey don't know what others say. If you do make changes to the company or policies, they won't know who was part of making these changes.

In recent years, we have also utilized Facebook polls in closed Facebook Groups or Facebook Pages. Facebook does not charge a fee for most polls and it gets you quick responses. These are good if you want the employees to see each other's answers to questions. This is very much transparent.

It is important to understand that you may hear some tough feedback, but Leaders need to HEAR the truth too. Just as, if not more important than being honest with your people and your customers, is taking their honest feedback to heart. We must be humble. We must be open to adjusting our plans.

Or, don't do anything and keep believing you are great as you are. That's what a lot of people do. They don't care what others think because they believe they are above criticism. That's why at the beginning of this book I mentioned that there are managers and there are leaders. Leaders tell the truth, and leaders listen to honest feedback.

One thing that will become glaringly obvious that things aren't going well, besides your bottom line, is turnover. Churn is a strong indicator as to your leadership. If your people know that you are willing to always listen to their feedback and suggestions, you could have a strong culture and business.

Another way that companies have gauged whether they are on the right track with their customer base, is through a Net Promoter Score, or NPS. The score range is Negative 100 (every respondent is a detractor) to Positive 100 (every respondent is a promoter). It serves as a barometer as to loyalty of your brand. When RE/MAX did this for the first time, my company score was a +75. Now that is higher than most Fortune 1000 companies that do this NPS, and was actually in line with where RE/MAX overall as a brand landed. BUT, as a leader I wasn't very satisfied, because I truly felt like we were capable of more, and anything less than a positive 100, does mean you are capable of improving. So, we used this score to invigorate us to find ways to do even better. We used the survey method to investigate what needed improving. After tweaking a few of the ways we interacted with our customers, we indeed did improve. In the next year's survey, we went up to a 95, which is unheard of. Building trust and loyalty with your team or with your customer is a constant leadership quality. Always strive to improve their experience and these different surveys are great ways to know where you stand.

Aside from surveying your people to improve your company, another thing that great leaders need to do, is offer feedback. We must offer immediate honest feedback. I have seen it all too often that managers will not share corrective criticism with their staff. Sometimes it is because they truly are afraid to do so because offering feedback or coaching someone can be challenging. I also have seen many managers not coach their staff in fear that the person might not like them as a manager or think they're mean.

I've learned years ago that it is way more important to be respected by your people than liked. This is an especially important concept to understand and live by. In my couple decades of leading companies, I have seen many managers go for the "like" factor, and more times than not, they don't make it. They fail. As opposed to being "respected." This leader is clear on expectations, and as a result, mostly avoids conflict. One of the most important statements I ever heard was that "Conflict only arises when expectations differ." Therefore, clarifying policies and setting clear expectations is a constant theme in this book. This all speaks to the *integrity* of a good leader. Adhering to strong moral and ethical principles and values.

Great leaders gain respect because they share feedback with their staff as promptly as needed. Respect leads to loyalty. Respect means that as a leader others will follow you.

If you are wondering whether you feel like having your people respect you versus like you is the right way to go, let me have you go through an exercise.

Don't limit yourself in your thinking when answering the following questions. If you think of world leaders, comedians, actors, athletes, teachers, family, friends, etc, put them down.

Make a list of the 10 people you respect the most in this world.

1. _____
2. _____
3. _____
4. _____
5. _____
6. _____
7. _____
8. _____
9. _____
10. _____

Then make a list of the 10 people you really like.
(Might be friends, family, musicians, actors, etc.)

1. _____

2. _____

3. _____

4. _____

5. _____

6. _____

7. _____

8. _____

9. _____

10. _____

Now, let's pretend that each one of the people you listed asked you to invest several thousand dollars of your hard-earned money into a new business they were starting. They also said that they plan to be the CEO of that company. Would you invest the money? Put a check mark next to everyone on both lists that you would invest your hard-earned money into. Now, let's pretend that each person asked you to quit working your current job or career and come roll the dice in this new business. Would you trust that you would be in good hands as an employee for them and that the business would grow and succeed for the long term? Put a 2nd checkmark next to the people that you ALSO would be ok trusting that they would lead a company to succeed. Now look at who you have two checkmarks next to. Likely you will have mostly people from the "RESPECT" list. There may be a couple on the "LIKE" list, but essentially this should further prove that it's better to be respected than liked.

The world is full of pretenders. Instead focus on leading with an honest heart and integrity. That will take you further up the leadership ladder.

I will say, that occasionally you will have someone that you both like and respect. That is possible for a leader as well. However, all I am saying is to aim to garner respect from your people FIRST. If they also then like you, then that's a bonus.

CHAPTER 5

Look in the Mirror

One of the things that has transpired over the years of me being a "manager" is that I realized many times when something went sideways, or did not go quite right, that it was my fault.

This concept of owning responsibility for the bad that happens just as much as the good is what I think helps shape great leadership. You see, we often feel like we can just get frustrated with staff when they don't do something correct. What do top leaders do? They internalize the idea of "looking in the mirror" FIRST.

Certainly, there are going to be mishaps and miscues. Some of your employees and sales reps that report to you will at some point mess up or do something outside of what's expected. I have ALWAYS believed though that their mistake, their miscue, could have been prevented. The question is, could it have been prevented by YOU or THEM?

Now hopefully when they started you set clear expectations and you trained them properly on the front end. In that case if they make a mistake, it may fall to them. I plan to share more on how to PREVENT mishaps by conducting proper training and development in later chapters.

But what if we did not give them the best training on the front end? What if it is our fault? I believe one of the best ways to tell whether you have management qualities or leadership qualities is whether you are able to analyze each circumstance to determine if there is something YOU could have done to prevent it from happening. Better training, more training, clearer expectations early on.

Let me give an example. Someone shows up late for work, time after time, and each instance they give an excuse of "traffic." "So sorry", they say, "but traffic was bad." Even in circumstances like this, you should ask yourself "Is there something differently I could have done to prevent this?" Ask this BEFORE getting upset and especially before implementing any potential corrective action.

Here is how to ask yourself: "Did I clarify the importance of being on time?" "Do we have policies in place to stress the importance of timeliness and our attendance policy?" "Do we even have an attendance policy?" AND, if we do have an attendance policy, "Did I go over it with them?" "Did they sign an acknowledgement of the policy?"

Looking in the mirror first at yourself, as a leader, will change the employee's perspective of you as well. They will start to respect you even more as a leader versus a manager. In the companies in which I've worked, I have had some of the lowest turnover of staff. I believe a huge part of why I had great success in low turnover, unlike many of my peers, is that I went through this exercise of assessing each circumstance of "Is it my fault, or the company's fault that THEY made a mistake?" I promise if this is your immediate first thought it will limit the conflicts and turnover that you have in your organization.

I think your staff sees that you care enough about them to not blow up, to not have a knee-jerk reaction to "writing someone up" just because they were late. I would literally share with my staff the following:

"So, this is the third time you've been late in the last 2-weeks. As I reflected on your training when you first started, I do remember clearly going through our attendance policy, but I am not one to just write someone up right away, so let me re-clarify that policy for you."

Sometimes after going through a recollection as to where did a breakdown occur, you'll realize that you do not have a policy but probably need one. In that circumstance, you should either suggest to HR or upper management that something gets put into place that helps clarify and possibly prevent more instances from happening, or if you own the business the bucks stop with you. You then need to take the time and/or hire someone to help create these policies. By the way, there are great Human Resource third party companies out there that you can hire that know local and state employment law and can help create a beautifully written employee handbook. That is exactly what we did at my companies to ensure adherence to the law and to stay up to date on current legal changes to employment law in my state.

With all this being said, I gave probably the worst example of when you should look in the mirror which is when someone shows up late. Typically, if someone shows up late, that is a character quality and not something that a policy can necessarily fix. However, I have learned through a couple decades of leading people, that if you take an extreme, like maybe being at fault for someone else showing up late to work, then the other more legit times when it can be your fault become clearer to see.

A different way to look at this, is to not point blame right away. If you plan to be a good leader and want to have loyal employees and a stronger company then you cannot point the finger too quickly. Always assume YOU messed up. YOU could have prevented the low sales of a salesperson on your team. You could have prevented the poor customer service and friendliness of your front desk person. You could have prevented them from mis-ordering key things for you or your business.

John C Maxwell stated in his book "Becoming a Person of Influence" that, "Instead of putting others in their place, put yourself in their place."

I remember years ago taking over a store for a large coffee company as the new Store Manager. The District Manager explained when they hired me that I was being given the responsibility of turning around profit on a store that had been four years in the red. You see this was one of their flagship stores in San Jose, CA. The founder of this fortune 500 company had always viewed this location as one of his most prideful stores. It was pertinent to turn this store around from being in the red to making money again.

Obviously the first thing I was to do was to analyze the Profit & Loss (P&L) for that location. I noticed a glaring line item where they were spending a lot of money, TRAINING. I came to realize that they had very high turnover. They were spending so much time and money on interviewing, hiring, and then training new employees.

I could not quite understand why they needed to turn so many employees so frequently. Then I realized after further evaluation that not enough of the right training was put into place to train properly and to help craft our people into a well-oiled machine. Whenever there was a breakdown in their day-to-day operations, management had constantly pointed the finger at the employees. The employees eventually got frustrated and quit. Or worse, management would make a quick judgement and fire people.

This not only effected staff morale for those remaining but also the customers coming in daily. They enjoy seeing employees who remember their names and remember their order. Hard to do if your staff constantly turns.

This became challenge number one for me. How do I limit the churn rate of employees and create better loyalty of our existing clients?

Well guess what? It starts with looking in the mirror. Now mind you, I had just joined this location. So when I say "mirror" in this circumstance, really, I am referring to the past management and the company. As the leader, the buck stops with me. We created better more thorough training programs on the front end so that our employees were efficient and effective in their roles.

I also wanted to ensure we had great development plans in place to allow current employees to be able to improve their skills and have the option of growing within the company. I felt like one thing missing before was the hope of further advancement from within. I helped turn that location around in only four months from red to black.

The company I was working for at the time was so grateful for the lessons they learned as well that they decided to create a new title for my role, "General Manager." Store Manager seemed too simple considering the capabilities of SOME of the Store Managers. And honestly, it provided a steppingstone between "Store Manager" and "District Manager." It essentially meant that you were running one of the more profitable stores or one of the more prominent in one way or another. Either based on location or sales volume.

My location became a desirable place for other employees throughout the company locally in my market. Many other Store Managers were bred from within my store. They were Assistants of mine that went on to run their own stores. The high morale that eventually transpired within my store also shined through to the consumer. We ended growing annualized sales as a result. We were able to lower churn of employees by clarifying expectations early through clear policies that we communicated. We were able to attract talent. Because others in our market got wind that we are a fast track to better roles within the company or into management. AND, we were able to influence our customer base to come more frequently as they enjoy seeing the regular employees. We also increased the store's average ticket (spend per visit) because customers were happier when they came. Increase morale of your employees and they will be loyal and follow you and the business to continued success.

All of this led to lower turnover, higher sales, and a much larger net profit for the company.

Years later I would go on to work for a competitor of this company and was asked to do the exact same thing. The new company asked me to run their main flagship store in downtown Seattle. At the time they suffered from almost the exact same thing, negative profit for years. Using a similar method as I had at my old company, I quickly implemented systems focused on training new employees right on the front end. I was able to turn that store around too from years in the red, to great returns in the black, in just 6 months. Look in the mirror first. I cannot stress this concept enough.

The industry took notice of some of my accomplishments and in 2004 I was recruited to work for yet another coffee company. This company was HUGE in California, but really had no presence in Washington. This would be their first coffee retail store in WA state and Seattle. They were very selective and flew me down to California to interview with the CEO. That led to me being selected from a nationwide search to open this first location in Seattle. They were nervous about this because Seattle at the time was dominated by Starbucks (headquartered out of Seattle). They literally told me, "Don't mess up. We NEED this location to work and be profitable if we are going to be able to succeed in Seattle." Luckily for me, we did succeed. It all started with recognizing that we all have faults. That if we start with creating great systems for ourselves, we can then implement to staff in order to build morale, limit turnover, and overall put yourself into a great position of becoming a great leader.

Going back to looking in the mirror. I think the best advice I can give in terms of succeeding as a leader in any industry is that when things go bad, assume it is your fault…because it is. And when things go well, give credit where it is owed. In all my examples above there are countless folks, colleagues and leaders above me, that crafted who I became. I never took credit for the successes of my individual locations. I could not have done it without several people's help. That is what leaders do. They recognize that their job is to create the plan and then lead with the plan. The actual work, the hard work, the grit, the service, is provided by the employees. It is easy to take credit for that work but instead, take credit for planning and work done on the front-end. Leave the remaining credit, you know the credit the public sees, to your staff or sales team. Humility will go far as a leader. Learn to be humble.

Whenever I saw another location in my company having success in a certain area or doing a unique thing that I felt I could implement better I would take that idea and implement it into my own location. Even though my stores or offices end up becoming one of the top in the company, it is because I add nuggets from several different stores to make mine better.

In real estate, it has been the same. I do not like reinventing the wheel. Every opportunity I get as a Brokerage Owner to network with peers or better yet, visit their offices, I take. I garner valuable ideas that can work at my company as well.

Want to move toward becoming a better leader? I highly recommend that you participate in brainstorming sessions with other peers in your field of work. At other branches or divisions within your company. In rare cases, even your competitors can bring great insight and assist you in becoming better. Join Facebook groups that can help you learn and also to improve your company, store, department or bottom line.

If you end up making a bad decision by implementing an idea you saw somewhere else, then look in the mirror again and take responsibility.

It is imperative that you coach and develop your executive team or other leaders in your company to also look in the mirror first. Think about it. If a mistake is made, the first level leaders will be trained to look in the mirror first. If they realize it is something THEY could have prevented, then it gets fixed and the staff then trained on the new way or policy.

This chapter can be wrapped up into the following: You are always responsible first. So, create the plan. Train to the plan. Develop others to use the plan. If any piece is not properly working. Look in the mirror first. Then revise as needed.

CHAPTER 6

Identifying Opportunity

O ne of the biggest differentiators between managers and leaders is that managers tend to stay within a framework. They don't venture outside the box that they are given. Some managers become very good at following rules, checking boxes, and in general grinding out the work each day. Great leaders know that there are always going to be hurdles. There are always going to need to be other ways to get to the finish line on a project or job. They always keep an open mind and many becoming very good at thinking outside the box.

One of the most valuable things that I personally have done as a leader, and then also watched several of my colleagues do, is to identify opportunities that can propel your business forward.

Let me start by saying that at one point in time at my company, I gave myself the title of "Director of Vision of Growth." Let us break down this title.

Vision is the direction you see the company going. Let's give some examples. In a real estate company it might mean sticking with just one office instead of expanding to another location. Maybe going deeper within my own office by increasing training and resources to the agents so that they sell more homes. Really trying to capitalize on the production of your current agents. That could be a vision for the company. Maintain your single office while improving the gross revenue per agent.

OR, your vision might be to expand your Brokerage, that currently is in just one city, to two or more locations in your respective county or province. For us, this was part of our vision. We started with one location in Everett, WA (just north of Seattle) and expanded to a second location and then on to a third and more. This might be your vision. To expand your footprint.

And then to the second half of my title, Growth. Growth also is reflected in the examples I gave above. Is the company poised to grow? Does it have the funds to expand? Does it have a foundation for growth? Do you know what that can look like? One of my mentors in life is Brian Buffini and he often says that if you don't build a solid foundation on a home, it will eventually crumble down. We must have a solid foundation for our company before we seek to grow.

Have you ever heard of a company that goes out of business and you ask yourself, "What happened, they were such an amazing company and always busy? Why did they go out of business?" Well, often it is because they grew too fast. No solid foundation before growing.

I recall being asked to speak at an international real estate conference on the topic of recruiting real estate agents. How do we do this successfully, and how do we grow. My very first point I shared was to not recruit until your culture was solid. It makes no sense to recruit several folks over to an environment that is toxic or negative. Start with your culture. Make sure that is foundationally solid. And then let's go recruit. We will talk more about culture later.

But back to this "Director of Vision & Growth" title I gave myself. I loved it because I really classify myself as a visionary. One that can see a future beyond our current circumstances. Often when I train on the topic of goal setting and creating a why the students struggle. They struggle because they are stuck in the mindset and thinking of their current circumstances.

As business owners and leaders, we must have the ability to dream beyond our current circumstances. In so many cases you are just one good idea, or one bold move away from massive success. Most people though are so afraid to be bold enough to dream that it stops them from pursuing their absolute best in business.

Therefore, I loved the title Director of Vision and Growth. I loved both aspects of the title. But what if an opportunity presents itself and it wasn't part of the original plan? This is why you are a leader. You must be able to see this as a huge plus for the company, even if it means redoing the budget, or going outside of the original plan you set for the year. Remember earlier when I stated Managers tend to stay within a framework? This is an example of expanding your thinking. Don't hold yourself and the company back by thinking, "Well that's just not in the plan." Think outside the box. Be bold and watch your career take off.

In my case, we became such a successful brokerage that other companies were approaching us to buy them out. At the time, our growth plans were to maintain current office count and create training and development plans to help our current agents and loan officers achieve more. In other words, go deeper with our current structure, not add more to it. The strategy we have been trained on is to go vertical not horizontal. (Go deep within, and not wide with more).

That said, we constantly had other office owners approach us and ask if we would be willing to buy them out. This was not typically planned for us to even look at these opportunities. But a true leader will not turn down an opportunity without first exploring the potential benefit to the greater good of their organization.

I understand that this could be scary, but you might be turning down something amazing, and so it is always worth at least exploring. My wife and I made offers multiple times on some of the opportunities that presented themselves. But it was rare that we acquired the right opportunity.

For us the right opportunity came in the form of our current franchise wanting to expand rapidly and so they offered incentives if we wanted to grow. Another couple of opportunities came when we were approached by no brand companies who were tired of the struggle of "How do I figure out running this tough business that is so competitive?"

You see, when you have laid a foundation yourself, created the systems that are working most flawlessly for you, then expanding or growing should be easy. I do need to caution, just like I did with my high producing agents back when they wanted to start a team…if you DON'T have structure, systems or right personnel laid out for your company, then you should be careful what opportunities you look at. In other words, do you have the funds to pull it off without crippling your company? Do you have reserves in case the new opportunity ends up costing you more than anticipated?

Being a visionary became an important part of our success in our companies. It's kind of like the gambler in Vegas, who knows when to hold 'em, and knows when to fold 'em. You must go with your gut just like that gambler. Much of the massive success that I've studied over the years have been from the owner or an executive having enough guts to at least look at the opportunities that present themselves.

You just need to know that by looking, you do not have to buy. Consider it your version of window shopping. You can look at all the goods, but you don't have to actually buy anything if you don't want to. Try on the outfit. If it doesn't fit, or you don't like the way it looks or feels on you, don't buy it. Same in business. Look at every opportunity, and even become known as someone who welcomes random opportunities. One offer or opportunity will lead to many more. Strike when it feels great and watch your business flourish, or…. DON'T. And stay where you are. This is what it means to be bold.

Fear is a tricky thing, and I have mentioned it already multiple times and will mention it again later. It can cripple you. Fear is dangerous. Be bold. Have the courage at least to explore. John Assaraf (Researcher, Author, and Entrepreneur) says, "A comfort zone is a beautiful place, but nothing ever grows there." If you want your company to grow, you've got to do some uncomfortable things.

Explore growth. Explore opportunities. Even explore the option of selling if someone approached you when you never even thought about selling your company. Be bold. You never know. My wife and I have been approached multiple times over the years about selling our firm. What we have found is that each time it makes us realize that we have something special. Something so special, someone else wants it. It drives us to do even more, grow even more, and help our agents grow further in their businesses.

I will also add another benefit to looking at expanding. Companies have certain key positions that they need whether they have one office or 10. My best example is a Bookkeeper, or Finance Manager. For a while when we were just one location, I did my own books but still hired a bookkeeper to help me balance the books and keep things straight. This was one of the many hats I wore. Once we opened a second office, we hired a full-time in-house bookkeeper. This position has morphed over time but the point is, that I still only have one full-time Finance person for all 5 of my locations. Same with a marketing person. You may pay someone to handle your social media or marketing related items. If you have one location, then this cost is high as a percentage of total revenue. If you have multiple locations, then this payroll cost gets spread out over multiple offices which reduces the overall cost per office, ultimately allowing more bottom-line profit.

If you haven't been convinced that looking at all opportunities is a good idea. Then at least consider what I just shared. The leverage aspect. We have taught for years that "Leverage is the key to success." Consider this: my salary as CEO, the Finance Specialist, the Transaction

Coordinator, and the Marketing Specialist are all able to be spread out over 5 locations. Ultimately making each location individually, more profitable.

To finalize my thoughts in this chapter, let me just say that sometimes you have to look for opportunities as well. At our company we once were warned that a clause in all of our franchise agreements was about to be enforced for the first time. It was a clause that dealt with the minimum number of agents you were required to have in your brokerage over time. For example, you must have 5 agents within your first year, 10 within two years, and maybe 20 by year three. But most brokerages ignored this clause and the company did not decide to enforce this, until recently.

In talking with our coach, we came to the realization that several of my local franchise owner colleagues would soon be faced with getting billed (fined) for not meeting their minimum agent count clause. So we created a plan to network with and grab coffee with the few folks in our market that we felt might be in harm's way of paying great fees for being under this count. In other words, do not be afraid to be proactive either.

If we just sit and wait for the possibility of the right opportunity, we may be stagnant in our growth. For me, I certainly am always hungry for maximizing our position in the marketplace.

What's the saying? "If you're not growing, you're dying."

CHAPTER 7

Leaders Seek to Grow Personally

You certainly want to make ensure you are not sugar-coating things within your work or business. Your people deserve the truth. And the truth, hard as it sometimes is to hear, is what helps people grow.

We have to also remember to tell the truth to ourselves. I have had the luxury of working with some of the most successful, amazing leaders at some top brands. I also know that top performers tend to let their ego get in the way of listening and growing themselves. I certainly have been suspect of this in the past myself. We need to ensure that we listen to suggestions from our people on ways to improve the company. It is often OUR opinion that no one will have better ideas than us. John C Maxwell says in his book Developing the Leaders around Yoy, "Every idea is a good idea, until we uncover the BEST idea." I love this. Being open to new ideas outside of our own is huge. Sometimes hard to hear that our idea was not the best. But it is for the good of the overall company to get several ideas and choose the best. Which might not be yours.

As stated earlier, we have utilized software like Survey Monkey to send out surveys to our people to get a snapshot of how we are doing and where we can improve. I think an essential attribute of great leadership is fully understanding the perception of your employees or customers. This is why so many companies these days offer surveys on their receipts after purchases. It is a real time snapshot of what's going on and maybe some weak spots in your organization. For me in my real estate and mortgage businesses, the surveys were geared towards what tools we should be providing our team or maybe where we should not be wasting money.

Perception is everything, and as a leader, we need to understand that OUR perception is only OUR perception. Our team or consumers perception of the training, of the product, of your tools, of your service, of your store or office interior, is what truly matters.

It is a humbling experience to bite your tongue and allow them to be honest and open in an anonymous survey.

In addition to understanding the true perception of your customer, you also need to be honest with yourself about where YOUR weaknesses are. We all have weaknesses. Putting yourself in a vulnerable position to discover what those are is a powerful thing. For example, maybe your weakness is follow-up. Maybe it's communication. Maybe it's organization. If you don't know through self-discovering, then ask a colleague, ask your employees, ask a close friend or your spouse. Then I would challenge you to ask yourself, "Based on what has been identified as MY weaknesses, what can I do to improve in that area?" I have found reading to be one of my favorite past times. I've created a self-assessment that I use and have recommended to help you dissect topics for learning.

I call it a "Personal Development Self-Audit". Essentially asking yourself, the following at the end of each year:

1. What skills did I learn this year that have helped me in my career?
2. What podcasts really brought great wisdom for my role in my company this last year?

3. What books did I read that inspired me to be a better leader?
4. What classes or conferences helped me to achieve great success in the past year?
5. What skills do I still need improvement in?

Investing time to reflect on the prior year and what transpired in the realm of personal growth can help you celebrate the growth while choosing appropriate development plans for the new year. I use this self-audit to help me choose topics for classes, books and podcast for the new year. Areas where I still need improvement. Great leaders are constantly striving to improve their shortcomings.

In general, I have found myself reading several books throughout the year as a result of these self-audits. Both in areas I already feel strong so that I learn a slightly different way to get even better results, and in areas where improvement is needed.

What book might you read that can help you to improve in a specific area? If you are not a reader, get the audio. Listen to it in the gym or on the way into the office. You also can listen to great podcasts on that topic as well. For example, if you were trying to improve your morning routine, then maybe subscribe to Hal Elrod's podcast on Miracle Morning. You can also attend seminars and trainings specifically on a topic. In the Real Estate industry, our agents take courses to earn Designations that help them become more specialized in an area they may be weak or desire more business or results. There is a designation one can earn called the RENE (Real Estate Negotiation Expert). Not only can one improve their negotiation skills but earning that designation and promoting yourself as having it can also create a boost in your conversion rates and higher sales.

I also want to discuss weaknesses as it pertains to your competitors. Likely you know what separates you from the competition. If you don't, not to worry, we will cover this in another chapter. But let's say you do know those weaknesses. I always like to ask myself if there is a way that I can capitalize on those weaknesses? Just because you are not weak in an area today, doesn't mean it won't grow to become a weakness. Learning by those around you also means identifying what your competitor is doing that their customers complain about.

I will discuss knowing your numbers in the next chapter but that comes into play here too. Not only knowing your own numbers but knowing the stats of the competitors. This will shine some gaping holes that might provide opportunity. Keep your eyes open.

Moral of this story is that improving in your weaknesses is better for your bottom line. Go humble yourself and find out what those areas are for you. And seek to improve yourself. Many leaders invest in a business coach and I am no exception. I would not be where I am today without the help and accountability of each of my coaches.

CHAPTER 8

Never Be Content & Know your Numbers

I am a competitive person as I believe all good leaders are. By nature, we tend to be competitive with our competition. We want to have #1 market share, be #1 in a specific category, or be the #1 department in our workplace. But being focused JUST on being #1 against your own competitor can be hurtful to a long-term strategy of tactics to accomplish it.

I have found over the years that we need to work on our own improvement first and grow against ourselves to have a chance of being #1 or beating the competitor down the street. The real measure should be against yourself. Therefore, for hundreds of years companies have used this as a way to measure growth. In a retail sales environment, they call it "comp" sales. How do they COMPARE to what they did last year? If you are beating last year's numbers, this is a good indication as to growth and some areas of success happening within your organization. If sales are down, you must course correct to identify WHY they are down so that you don't slowly find yourself out of business.

Statista.com shares a telling story of business bankruptcies in the United States. In 2019, it was almost 23,000 businesses that didn't make it. I can assure you that several 1000's of these businesses could've prevented bankruptcy had they been better not only at tracking their numbers but using them as a tool to understand the weaknesses of the business. For some businesses, it was a lack of finding a cost-effective way to make their product or do their service. This would've shown in their ability to track their top line revenue, minus COGS (Cost of goods sold) which then leaves their net revenue. The net revenue is what's left to run the business.

In most businesses, the largest expenses are in the Rent / Lease of space and in their payroll costs. So again, if revenue, and / or profit is not where it needs to be…then are we too heavy in payroll or rent? Is the space we are renting too big? Can we find a slightly smaller space that still allows us to function? In recent years retailers have taken a beating from online retailers and companies like Amazon. Controlling your leasable square footage is going to be key if you are in a retail environment. Leaders help identify these things as well. It's common that the owner of a company doesn't frequent the business. So as leaders we need to help identify these lost opportunities of saving money for the company. Again, I think this is a differentiating point. If you manage a department or a retail store or restaurant and you see waste, are you reporting it or making suggestions to save the company money?

Have you ever had the thought, "They don't pay me enough to make those types of decisions?" If you have had that thought, then that could be why you are in that position and not being promoted or given larger raises. Leaders put others first. Including the company's best interest, before their own. I promise you that if you show a desire to always be helping, always be sharing, and giving of yourself, then success will come to you. You will be identified as a worthy leader.

At the beginning of the book, I told you about my personal story of entering into real estate as a brokerage owner. It was in August 2008.

Towards the beginning of the Great Recession. I had found a tiny office space to start at and signed a one-year lease. After a year I made the mistake of moving to a larger prominent location that was hopefully going to get me more exposure. Here is a lesson on exposure I learned the hard way. Exposure can also be bad. Because once I realized this nice office location that had a high lease payment was too much for me to afford, I had to beg the landlord to let me out of my lease. This was now right smack in the middle of the Great Recession, and my lack of personal home sales weren't helping my cause either. But I was constantly analyzing my numbers to see what I could do to improve my position. Sometimes you can't control the outside environment, but you better find a way to control your inside environment, or you will be out of business. That landlord, thank god, let me out of my lease. When I moved to a new smaller location, on the 4th floor of a building, I had lost some respect of the community. Why? Because they saw this exciting new office come into town, on a busy road, but then have to close just a year later. That is why sometimes great exposure, can be bad exposure.

Also, when it comes to staffing, you may identify that payroll is what's holding you back from being profitable. The "people" line item is two-fold. First, do you have too many employees? Or are you paying them too much? (market rate) Second, are they being utilized correctly or to their best capabilities?

You see, you don't have to automatically go to a place of layoffs. You can see if maybe you switched what that person did can they provide better, more profitable results for the company? I'm recommending that you not go straight to a place of layoffs because I have also learned the hard way that Hiring and Re-Training a new person is more costly than just course correcting the person's duties or increasing their production. If you then cannot get more out of them to help your bottom line, the decision can be made to lay them off.

SCOTT COMEY

Analyzing the numbers. So incredibly important. At a minimum, once per month review your numbers. Where are you spending and where are you making your money. Then a minimum of twice a year, run some numbers on your competitors. This gives you a bi-annual snapshot of where you are compared to them.

My wife used to work for a large retail chain, and did you know that these large retailers do price comparisons all the time against each other? They actually send in people with price scanners to scan key products (common type items) to see what their competitor in that specific local community location is charging. That way they can course correct if they are way out of line. Not that price is the only factor, but you will be quickly out of business if you are way out of line on pricing as a retailer. Target and Wal Mart have been doing this for years, and they are both still around, and both very strong financially. Both companies know their personal value and their demographic, but they also analyze their competitor's pricing strategies frequently.

Knowing the numbers is only valuable if you do something with this knowledge. I had this concept I internalized of never being content. In our annual Award's Banquet, I took pride in sharing with the entire company and in front of their spouses and guests, all of the great accomplishments we had in the prior calendar year. We would be #1 in this and #1 in that. It got them all fired up to repeat it again in the new year. But imagine a scenario whereas the leader you say, "I'm #1, so I can finally not work so hard." Believe it or not, some companies are this way. Some leaders can't even tell you how they became #1. For me, I was never content. Being #1 is scarier than being #2. There is pressure to not lose it. And the leader that embraces this idea, will likely find ways to improve against themselves, year after year, and just continue to create separation as the years go by.

I often think about the drivers in NASCAR. In many races, the leader often is in that position for several laps. Sometimes over 100 laps. If that driver isn't constantly thinking about how to improve and stay

#1 they can get passed on the track. The drivers often rely on data, like their own lap times and the lap times of the competitor in the #2 and maybe even #3 position. As long as the driver can continue to improve their own lap time, or at least improve above the lap time of the cars behind him / her, then they will win the race.

In watching the Tour de France, it never ceases to amaze me that the rider who is #1 and is constantly looking back at the rider behind him, eventually gets passed. Instead of focusing on improving yourself and watching the numbers that your team occasionally shares from the side of the road or with a passing car and a chalk board with data. Basically, I am just trying to share the extreme importance of knowing what your competitors are doing. Are they improving in certain areas, or not? You must have a pulse on your competitors and your industry trends. With us, we have five offices, and so we do track even each individual location against its top 6-10 competitors.

Apple and Amazon are two companies that are great examples of never being content and creating further separation within their space.

I was working at Crown Books back in 1997 in Silicon Valley. The internet boom was starting to pick up and we were quickly approaching Y2K. Amazon was founded just a few years prior in 1994. I remember learning about this new company that was going to revolutionize book buying in the future. In just a short period of time, I received notice from Crown Books Corporate that we were in financial turmoil as a company and I as a Store Manager was tasked with reducing my staffing by 40%. Talk about tough decisions a leader has to make. I never wish this on anyone, which is why I really state the fact of know your numbers. This is true for you as a Team Leader of a sales team. Know your numbers. Crown Books, a nationwide book retailer for decades, did not analyze their numbers quick enough to make any changes to their sales tactics, and eventually went out of business as one of Amazon's early victims. It was tough being in this position back in the day, although very insightful to witness firsthand.

It's amazing how lessons can be learned during turmoil too. Fast forward a couple decades later and Barnes and Noble is still in business. Why? Because they did analyze their numbers and created a game plan to respond to this new competitor, this new disruptor of the book sales industry. The flat-out fact is that bookstores require large footprints to display their books, and many people to keep those displays looking good. Amazon of course, is online, so they just need marketing and tech folks, warehouse workers and nationwide customer care. Even many of their "warehouses" are individual sellers throughout the nation housing the books in their own stores, or garages. Brilliant. Much easier to be profitable in a more virtual environment versus brick and mortar.

As time has gone by, large retailers like Barnes & Noble, Target, Wal Mart, etc. have adapted and have amazing online platforms now that compete with Amazon. But Amazon has this mentality of never being content. In 2016, Amazon had just shy of $136 Billion (with a "b") in revenue, and $2.37 Billion in net earnings. Just a few short years later, they had more than doubled in revenue to over $280 Billion, and net earnings of $11.59 Billion. Jeff Bezos had really analyzed the numbers to create a plan to not only stay #1 in their space, but further the gap between their company and others. Through crunching the numbers during this timeframe, they also found ways to increase their bottom line by almost 5 times. I don't know too many folks that would believe such a multiplier would've existed in a company that large, but they did it. You think knowing your numbers are important?

So why did Amazon dominate so quickly early on in the book space? One of the reasons was that reading paper books was statistically declining as technology improved over the years. Also, the need to come into a physical location was also declining as consumers had easier ways to now research book titles and even reviews. It could be said that the bookstores did not adapt to a somewhat aging consumer base. Jeff Bezos once said, "If your customer base is aging with you, then eventually you are going to become obsolete or irrelevant. You need to be constantly figuring out who are your new customers and what are you doing to stay forever young." Even those these big retailers I mentioned, Target, Walmart and Barnes & Noble currently seem to be handling the online transition that has limited in person sales from year's past, there are no guarantees that they will remain profitable or even in business in the future.

If you currently are a manager desiring to move into true leadership, then embracing this concept of "Never being content" will gain much respect. From the owners and Executives above you, to your peers, and also to your employees.

CHAPTER 9

Leading Through Challenging Times

I n your tenure as a leader there most certainly will be challenging times. In fact, likely several. Some may be your own making, and some will be outside of your control. When I used to sell homes for a living as a Realtor, my clients would often ask me, "Scott, do you think this home will continue to increase in value over time?" You see, even as an advisor or a salesperson, you are a leader. Your client, the consumer, is expecting to look to you for advice.

I always had great responses to this question, in good economies and bad. This is another way to become a leader. Anticipate the questions that might get asked of you and practice them frequently. Or, if you anticipate objections, practice how you will respond so you aren't having to figure out a response in front of the person. At RE/ MAX, where my wife and I own multiple offices, we bought into a training program years ago called "Momentum." In Momentum, we talk about having "Tool Belt Dialogues." Essentially what this is, are dialogues you can pull out and use, should you need them. Like a contractor on a job site who wears a toolbelt. He may not need all of those tools today, but because he may not know which one he may need today, he brings multiple tools to be prepared. Same goes for anticipating what may be asked of you. Create your own dialogues for responses to those questions so that you are fully prepared.

Back to the question I used to get asked from my homebuyers about whether the value of the home they were thinking about writing an offer on would continue to increase in the coming years. In good economies, I would answer that question like this, "The market is strong right now, and likely will remain strong for years, however; I don't have a crystal ball." I went on to remind them of two powerful things that can change even the strongest of economies, "Even though we all expect the market to stay strong, it can change quickly if there is a natural disaster, or world event." Being from the west coast, and spending my entire life there, I have personally been through many earthquakes, and if they are strong enough, they do affect the economy, and most aspects of business. The severity is dependent upon the level of quake.

My wife and I also own a home in South Carolina, and in our short few of years there, have been through two hurricanes. If you've never been through a Hurricane, let me give you a quick insight. The Governor of each state affected, typically at some point orders an evacuation, because the good news about Hurricanes is that there is commonly plenty of time to prepare. With evacuations, businesses get shut down and people leave town. The economy is affected. Also, depending upon if it was a direct hit or how long the flooding that happens afterwards lasts, it can devastate local economies. The same would be the case for Tornadoes, Tsunamis, Avalanches, Volcanic Eruptions, Major Fires and more. So, YES, this unpredictable event can most certainly change even the strongest economies, and this is out of our control.

In addition, there are world events that can happen and affect our economy. When I used to tell my clients about world events, I would speak mostly about the possibility at any moment that our country may go to war. Our country historically cannot seem to get through an entire decade without being involved in a war, and that does tend to effect economics. Again, depending upon the severity of the war. Another world event that we are currently in as I write this book, is the COVID-19 Global Pandemic. The country is currently shut down. Prior to this COVID-19 finding its way into our country in early 2020, the country was having record years in GDP growth. The real estate market nationally was on pace for a record year and already had an amazing January and February, but then this Pandemic. Fast forward to stay home orders, more than 90% of businesses being forced to close, the airline and cruise industries being devastated, unemployment at almost 40% and at an all-time high, and you are quickly in a new challenging world.

The point here is don't get too comfortable with current circumstances. Things can change literally overnight, whether world event, or natural disaster. Always be prepared. I once heard a quote on a podcast that I love. "Always be worried when things are at their best." Now, you can get what you want out of this quote, but what I heard was, "be prepared". Don't be content. And always have a plan. For us and our business, that plan mostly included financial reserves. I will discuss more about this a bit later in the chapter.

Crisis will challenge you to the core. Both personally and professionally. I told our company this early on when the Pandemic was first announced. It will make or break you as a person. Martin Luther King once said, "The Ultimate Measure of Man is not where he stands in moments of comfort, but where he stands at times of challenge and controversy." I LOVE this quote. A good leader will embrace a challenge and not run from it, or curl up in the fetal position. But here's the challenge for you? Your people may curl up. Just be prepared to meet each person where they are. They don't want to be managed during this time. They want to be led. They need direction. They need to be assured that you and the company have things under control.

As I am writing these words, the country is also going through yet another challenge. Racial Injustice and the recent death of a black gentleman named George Floyd. George was murdered by a white police officer and it sparked protests, riots, looting and a revisit to the racism problems in our country. Social media has been lit up with posts and comments about this event. Events like this divide further an already divided country.

We have seen many leaders make comments about it. It appears they feel like they have a moral obligation to address it. I feel like sometimes leaders feel they have a box to check with something so controversial as this. It honestly is sad. Many CEO's quickly made statements or released letters on company letterhead stating something along the lines of, "Our company does not condone racism, and we believe racial inequality needs to stop. This was a horrific death, and we stand for justice." I can literally see the CEO's check that box off of their "to-do" list.

Real leaders, the good leaders, will truly lead from the heart. They will stand for their principles, and in fact, reflect on how a tragedy comes into play with their Mission / Vision / Core Values. The better leaders of today, I have witnessed, step up. Action is sometimes what's needed by leaders, not words on a page, or even spoken words, but action.

After going through multiple crisis with our businesses, we have identified four primary categories where you need to ensure you have a plan, in order to lead effectively during them. I have an acronym I will use here called F-O-M-O. Several of you will recognize this as commonly standing for, "Fear Of Missing Out." But we cannot fear a challenge. And we certainly cannot afford to miss embracing challenge and potentially coming out of it stronger than you went into it. No, I'm talking about Financial—Organizational—Mindset—Operational. Four categories to focus on to create a solid plan to keep you leading through and out of a crisis. F-O-M-O.

Financial—In a crisis it is imperative that as a leader you ensure you are poised to sustain the rough waters that may be ahead for your company. As I mentioned earlier, number one on your list is to ensure reserves for your company. Now, I am creating this segment of the book, not as a reference guide for WHEN a crisis occurs, but rather as a checklist of things to help you create the game plan for if / when it occurs, you and the business are prepared. When I say you need to ensure your business has reserves, I mean prior to a crisis. If you don't have reserves, create a game plan to get you to 3 months and eventually to 6 months of reserves.

That starts by working on saving the first 3 months. If your business or department costs $20k a month to cover overhead, then start by saving $60k. (3 months of expenses). After you are comfortably at 3 months of reserves in savings, move to save another 3 months' worth, so that you have 6 months reserves. Obviously, this is separate from any funds you personally have saved, or assets. We are talking mostly about liquid reserves, easily accessible if needed.

No matter what your industry, if you have 3-6 months of reserves, you should be able to weather most storms since in most cases you likely will still have ways to produce some income. For a longer recession, like the Great Recession, having more will help immensely. Since typically during a recession your sales don't go to ZERO, even 6 months of reserves should last you well beyond 6 months. Now, I'm not a financial advisor, but make sure you have one that can help advise you as to whether this money should truly be in savings or be in some other financial vehicle that is somewhat liquid but moving the company towards a better return on the money. There are also some financial advisors that will tell you to save 9 months or even a year or more of savings towards reserves. You may also find a combination of cash reserves and credit availability to be suitable for emergencies. I'm not a fan of credit for the wrong reasons, but it certainly can be helpful in the right circumstances. One of the things that helped me get through the Great Recession was a line of credit through my business bank account. I am giving only the advice of the years of reading and studying that I have done and the advice we give to the independent contractors at our company.

Another important aspect is to ensure you are always operating off a budget. Good leaders with strong financials do not veer outside of a budget. In other words, we create a mindset of, if I want something today that was not on the budget then I need to remove something of equal expense that was on the budget. That is what running a tight budget means. Get yourself a solid business budget if you do not currently have one. If you do have one and a crisis happens, you need to immediately look at the budget and see if there are items that can be removed or slimmed down. One of the best things we have done since this Pandemic has hit, was identify some recurring charges on our bank statements of items that we truly did not need anymore. You know, the items that are $20 or $50 or $100 a month which sounded like very little at the time, and now you've been being charged for them for potentially years but the value of what you get just isn't relevant anymore? Those. Get rid of them. By the way, do this personally, and encourage your employees to do the same on their home budgets so that they too are better prepared to weather this storm as best they can. Speaking of educating your own people, we ended up creating two separate financial workshops to help our people because we really felt like the better we can help them personally with budget and spending, then the less they will rely on us as a company should we need to cut their hours, etc.

I do want to caution you to be very mindful of anything you decide to cut from the expenses during a crisis because it could have a negative effect and hurt you more. For example, really analyze the return on investment (ROI) of something before cutting. If it something that is helping to create more income to your bottom line, don't cut it just because it seems like a good amount of money will free up, because you will be adding insult to injury of the circumstances.

Organizational—From an organizational standpoint, you always want to ensure you only have staff that are contributing to the company in one fashion or another. If you ever have the thought, what does this person really do for us? That's when they likely shouldn't be with you anymore. Constantly analyzing this is especially important, so that if a crisis does occur, you aren't more devasted. We personally love our people and layoffs is a word I really don't like, so if we had dead weight prior to a crisis, I would hate to let someone go who should've been let go well before that. But once a crisis occurs, it is imperative that you look at all personnel and not make too quick of decisions to layoff. That can have a devastating impact on many things. Public perception of layoffs can look like your company is in turmoil, maybe well before it truly is. Also, that person, may end up finding another job, and even if you felt like the layoff would be temporary until things get better, the employee may not be available anymore and we all know how hard it is to find good help. Lastly, laying off with an absolute intent to rehire once the economy gets better can cause more hiring and training costs and ultimately make matters worse long term than just finding a way to keep that person employed. So, no knee jerk reaction to laying off. Not to mention the stress on you as a leader in having to find a replacement when the time comes and figure out training to hope they end up being as good as the person you laid off.

Mindset—I believe mindset to be the single most important segment of winning during challenging times. We must start re-dedicating ourselves to our Mission / Vision / Value / Beliefs as a company. How can we be triumphant in making it through a crisis? We need to look to our MVVB. Can our Mission Statement or Vision Statement pull us through? And if so, in what ways? Before totally writing a new script, and redoing your entire budget, you must make sure that the changes you make do not affect your MVVB. In addition, there will be crisis that come along, where your MVVB is going to help create the plan to get you through.

As I mentioned, Racial Injustice has become another challenge in society today due to the recent murders of black citizens by police officers. Employees from companies have looked to their leaders for a statement, and as I mentioned earlier, most larger companies came out and made one. Or they created a letter for press release saying how sorry they are for what had happened, and condolences for the families of those killed. But this has been part of the problem for centuries. Too many words and not enough action. When my wife and I decided it was time for us to respond to these same circumstances, we looked at our MVVB. And our Core Values stood out to us. Specifically, "Personal Growth", "Character" and "Community". Those are three of our Core Values. Personal Growth because it helps with educating the mind. With mindset. How can we better learn WHY this continues to happen so that we can help create a plan to do our part as a small company to make a change. Character, because we only hire people we believe have good character. If we sense they do not, then they are not a good fit for our culture. We must do unto others as we would like done unto us. The Golden Rule. Last, Community. Now more than ever our community is crying for help. Permanent help to address long needed changes in society.

Our Mindset, our Core Values, led us to create a letter that went out to both of our companies, followed by a plan to address change and a LIVE Facebook video to our people. We felt it important for them to SEE the pain of the tragedy on our faces and see that we actually intend to make change. In our case, we decided to have an open discussion session via webinar to discuss any biases or racism that any of us have felt before. We made it clear that there will be no judgement and no recording. After we listen, we will create a plan to move towards making a change. Together, we will decide as an organization with all people's opinion's involved, the action we will take to do our part.

That is what leadership is all about. Taking a stand and taking action. There have been several leaders, including peers of mine, that did remain silent, in fear they might say the wrong thing. I am here to tell you, that if you lead from the heart, and you tell the truth, you cannot do wrong.

To further discuss why MINDSET is such an important element of leading through a crisis, let me tell another story. In 2008, I started my Real Estate Brokerage, "Real Estate Bundle" and by 2009 we were still in the Great Recession. I knew that my attitude would affect those around me, so I did what I could to focus on what I could control and not the things out of my control. I certainly was not going to wait and see what the government would do for me and my business. By the way, quick side note. That is NOT a plan. Relying on the government during times of crisis, is not a plan. So, rule #1, create a mindset where others bailing you out is not an option. Therefore, you must create the plan yourself. That's a mindset choice.

By "others" I mean…Not your parents, Not your rich friend, Not the Government and Not the parent company of your Franchise. If any of them eventually offer help, great. But, relying on it as part of a plan you must avoid.

When this Global Pandemic first came about and started to affect our business, I was overly concerned about how our people will react. Everyone tends to take these serious events differently and so that is the first thing I learned, was to embrace the fact that everyone will be in a different place with this. It is our job as leaders to not judge and to meet people where they are.

My wife and I have been maintaining a positive mindset. This does not mean you need to be cheerful and excited. Maintaining a positive mindset means you are not going to let the negative things happening around you affect your mindset. Often this involves removing yourself from watching or listening to the news. The news is designed to cause drama and to negatively challenge our minds, so stay away from it. If as a leader you need to stay up to date on the local things as it pertains to your crisis, limit yourself to 30 min MAX a day to get a quick update.

With the Great Recession, I hosted monthly meetings for me people. In those meetings I would share local market stats so that they had talking points to use for their clients since so many consumers were constantly concerned about "How's the market?" In a Recession, there typically are not a ton of great stats that would give consumers hope, so I only tended to share with my people the positive stats, which there ALWAYS are in any circumstance. I would say for every 6 bad stats, there was maybe one good one, but sharing that one good one, gave hope. During crisis, it is easy to be consumed into the negative spiral, and if you focus on the negative stats, it can cause your mind to go to some bad places, which may make you think, there's no hope, I'm going out of business. Keep your mind clear by focusing on Positives. I promise that it will carry you and your people forward. If you dwell on the negatives, so will your people, and it will trickle down and effect the bottom-line. Do your best to keep spirits up as hard as that can be, trust me.

One of the things my wife and I got good at recently during this global pandemic is morning routines. Crisis can allow you to build new habits, so capitalize on it. Use a negative circumstance as an opportunity to build. Build yourself and build your people. Our morning routine was adapted from Hal Elrod and his book Miracle Morning. He has a "30-Day Challenge" which includes a SAVERS routine. I won't get into detail with this so go read the book, it's amazing. Essentially, we do quick workouts in the morning, along with Silence / meditation, reading daily, journaling daily, and saying affirmations to yourself while visualizing your goals in life.

This routine really helped with mindset for us. You may ask, what did we read during this time? Books that added to maintaining a positive attitude. Self-help books and business books that helped me keep my mind strong. We also listened to podcasts that kept our mind moving forward on solutions versus dwelling on the problems.

Lastly, we doubled down on networking with our peers. Through Facebook groups we have been able to keep our own spirits high, by seeing what our peers were doing so we weren't having to totally re-invent the wheel and know we weren't alone.

OPERATIONAL

During a crisis, it is important to assure that some necessary measures are taken to most protect the organization and the building(s) in which it resides. Analyzing, for example, if security measures need to be taken for any of your locations. If a natural disaster, was their structural damage that may lead to further damage or looting? Secure all entry points and consider installing cameras for security reasons if it is within your budget. We installed multiple cameras during COVID-19 pandemic and the "Stay Home" orders.

For any marketing that was happening, consider if it needs to be paused or increased. During the COVID-19 crisis, I have been witnessing some amazing ads hit billboards and commercials via radio and TV. A strategy around your ongoing marketing should be put into place. Delivering the right message to your primary customer is key.

Think if there is anything else that may need to be looked at? For us, during the COVID-19 health crisis, we purchased and provided several hand sanitizers in all our offices and provided protocol to be followed by all our staff. We also installed signs throughout each location reminding everyone of the sanitizing protocols to keep our offices safe and as sanitized as possible to help prevent further spread of the disease.

PERSONAL DEVELOPMENT DURING A CRISIS

A personal plan for self-improvement is key during a crisis. We have the unique ability to also grow during a crisis. If there is a to be a silver lining, it would be this. The first question you need to ask, is what do I need to learn about with what just happened that could make me a better leader? If it was an earthquake, maybe reading up on how past earthquakes effected businesses and what they did for that specific disaster to move forward and get to a spot of reopening.

When the Great Recession happened in 2008/09, I quickly became somewhat of an economist, reading up and educating myself to help with a plan for my business and for educating the people that relied on me for valuable and pertinent updates. I did the same in 2020 with the COVID-19 crisis. I taught myself all about Recessions and what causes them and how economies recover from them. During COVID-19, I didn't want to rely on my own experience or knowledge to get through something so devastating, so almost all of the books I've been reading have been to help me be a better leader, stronger mindset, and keeping a positive attitude. This is mostly because during any crisis, people get panicked and scared, and typically lose hope, especially if their income is affected, which it commonly is. If I can learn how to maintain a positive attitude during a time of crisis, then I now become a resource for those in my employment.

During this recent COVID-19 crisis, I was listening to a podcast from the National Association of Realtor's Economist sharing what he was reading, which were books on Economics. Funny right? The leading economist in the United States for Real Estate and he decides of all the books during this crisis that he is diving deep into learning more about his profession?

And that is my point. Start with reading, listening to, or watching to learn more about how to handle and come out of whatever crisis you are faced with. Next step would be to utilize any spare time, which may or may not be available with a crisis, to improve other skills you have been wanting to improve but had not had the time to.

Remind yourself in any crisis that people have lived before you and likely have answers to many questions that you have. I live on the principle of NOT reinventing the wheel. I also tend to plug into webinars and trainings that companies put out during this time. Companies that have way more experience than I on handling these things. So, plug in. If you belong to a Franchise company, plug in to everything your company is offering. Read every email they send you. If you do not have this luxury, then sign up for updates from trusted sources that can quickly get you information you need. During the recent Pandemic, we became members in NFIB. Not that I am advocating for you to consider joining them, but organizations like that make it their fulltime job to keep small businesses informed. They can eliminate a bunch of research you would've had to do and don't have time to as it pertains to how businesses are being affected, etc.

One last thing I will mention under Personal Development is to encourage all the above for your people. If you have a sales team, like I do, then make sure to pass your tips and resources on to them so that they too can be better prepared for their own clients when they get asked for advice.

There are many other elements on this topic, as it pertains to improving during crisis. But that can be for another book. This will get you and your people started.

Reference this section of the book if / when you must deal with a crisis yourself, but at least you have a few ideas for how to quickly get a plan in place should you face one.

CHAPTER 10

Leading Through Video

Gosh, where do I start with talking about video and leadership? I have recently become a student of video and wanting to improve my own game in this category. I find it to be incredibly powerful in leadership specifically. I have been hearing "use video" for years now, but never got huge onto that band wagon. Neither has most of the population. Well, about two years ago the leader of RE/MAX LLC, CEO Adam Contos, created a closed Facebook Group for owners / leaders in his network. The next thing I knew, he was posting video after video, and almost two years later, has not stopped. I believe he averages two a day now. LIVE videos at that.

Up to this point, I had mostly done video through email using Bomb Bomb. Bomb Bomb is a cool software program that allows you to send video through email and track the open rate, and so much more. It has become one of my favorite tools because it is so easy to use and a huge aspect of my success as a leader. Well, Bomb Bomb did an event in Denver in May of 2019 called "Re-Humanize." The event was also a launch of a book written by two Executives at the company. What was this amazing book? "Re-Humanize Your Business" by Ethan

Beute and Stephen Pacinelli. If you aren't familiar with the company Bomb Bomb, check it out. They have mastered the art of delivering exceptional customer experiences and these two leaders at the company are a huge part as to why.

I was given that book by a great friend and colleague of mine, Zach Hensrude, who had been growing his own knowledge of the power of video and thought it could benefit me and our company as well. I also received it again for attending the seminar and despite the fact that it should've been a sign that I need to read this book, it instead sat on my bookshelf for a year.

As the days went by, I continued to see Adam Contos' videos, day in and day out. I decided, ok, if he is believing in video so much, then maybe I need to become a student and learn more about it. So I read the book, and OMG. If you want to quickly learn about what to do, what not to do, how to capitalize and improve open rate, and so much more...then read the book. They even touch on what to say in the subject line of emails. Multiple tips and ideas to help with engagement. The best thing the book reveals is that video allows you to connect and get to know people through video. So much so, that when they meet you for the first time, they feel like they know you already. They share several examples of this in the book, so go check it out.

As leaders, we really want instant reception of the message we are trying to get across in emails and since emails are often interpreted incorrectly, video can be a time saver for you. In the book they talk about the power of Face to Face. Another true differentiating point between managing people and leading people, is getting to fully understand and know your people. You can do this through video and face to face interactions. Versus just plain old emails.

"Before you click send, post, or publish next time, ask yourself, would this be better if I said it face to face?" (Excerpt from the book) If you want a quick snippet of what the book is about, or a few tips on video, check out my podcast "Turn the Dial" episode 39 is an interview with one of the authors, Ethan Beute from Bomb Bomb.

Back to Adam Contos. Of all the CEOs I have worked under over the years, I have never had a leader so engaged with his people and so accessible, than Adam. Or at least my perception was that he was accessible. Almost all of his videos were LIVE, so they were raw. I really started to grow a connection with Adam through video. In fact, I love so much how he was leading with Video that I asked him to be a guest on our Podcast. I specifically asked him why it is important for him to be transparent and connected with his people. I think often we grow so much professionally that those under us think we are hard to reach or even have a conversation with. This is why I wanted to become a student of video and learn all I can about why it is a valuable tool in business today, especially for leaders. I wanted to be more visible like Adam. Leading the video charge through his own actions. By the way, he also asks those under him to commit to the same. And now, other Executives at RE/MAX have been utilizing video frequently. Leading by example, I love it. As a result of this level of commitment to video, RE/MAX grew to the largest agent count in the history of the company, and quite quickly.

I mentioned that video can show you as the leader, raw. It shows your imperfections. It shows your mistakes. It shows that you are real, which is the most desirable aspect of growing in a relationship. Have you ever heard of something or someone being "scripted"? Does not sound appealing right? I challenge you when you start in video, just let the mistakes shine through. Your engagement with the video will be even better. In the book RE-Humanize, they state "Our imperfections are our perfection." They suggest when you record a video, don't re-record it. Send it.

In 2020, during the Racial Injustice protests and riots, my wife and I were leading a somewhat divided company on many things that were happening in the world. On top of these riots and looting, there was the Global Pandemic, and oh yeah, a Presidential race going on as well. Our companies had many varying emotions. I mentioned earlier how my wife and I addressed to our companies our response to Racial Injustice, and that we intended to take action on something within our company to do our part. But we had not gone public with any statement yet to the consumers, and to the world. Well, I decided that someone needed to tell other leaders that we cannot just respond with just a letter. We cannot just respond to a crisis with spoken words that mean nothing. For words to really mean something there has to be action behind them. And so talk about raw, I decided to put myself out there. On Facebook LIVE, and without stopping, editing or re-recording, I went on for about 8 minutes and mentioned how we all need to step up and lead by making change. To not think small, and to know that ANYTHING you can do, is worth doing to help solve the issue of Racial Injustice. It literally does take everyone doing their part. And with something that has lasted for more than a century, it likely will take everyone doing something.

I can tell you that the text messages, comments, Facebook private messages that I received from so many people was uplifting to me as well. Because even though I knew I had to lead from my heart, and I certainly needed folks to SEE the emotion on my face so that they grasped the severity of the crisis and the importance to me as a leader, I was still nervous that maybe I offended someone. Maybe it costs me losing someone from my organization. I mentioned in my video that there may be someone wanting to leave my employment after watching, and you know what, I'm ok with that. I think having a firm stance also is key to leadership. People need to know what you stand for, and in video they not only see it, they can feel it through your emotions. I want you to ask yourself this question: When times get tough and when the world around us is struggling, do we want to manage our people? Manage their expectations? Or lead them through the challenge? No one is saying that it will be easy and trust me it was not, but the respect gained by taking some action is what can separate you from being a "Manager" to being a "Leader."

To give you another example as to the importance of being raw, let me tell you about my brother Dustin and something he did when was first getting into video. He shared how his most popular video that gained the most "LIKES" and engagement, were the blooper videos he did. That's because people like that you are real and that you actually make mistakes. I know some leaders think that they want to have the perfect makeup, be wearing the perfect clothes, and have an outline for their video that was perfectly scripted. And that is the only way they will do the video. The problem lies in the execution. Most likely that video is not getting done. And if it does, I can promise you that your competitor likely has done 4-5 videos in the same amount of time. Remember Ethan Beute from Bomb Bomb whom I mentioned above? He wears a t-shirt in many of his videos. An Executive in a t-shirt? Yep. You think his employees love that about him? Absolutely. He is relatable. No stiff collared button up on this guy, and that is partially why is a great leader. He is himself and it shows through the videos he does.

There is a National Speaker / Coach that several high performing Executives and salespeople follow named Jon Cheplak who says, "My crappy video is better than your non-existent one." And so as a leader, I highly recommend looking into doing regular videos to your team. For my wife and I, we mostly accomplish this through a closed Facebook group. Between her and I we are doing a LIVE video on there about three to five times a week. In addition, our leadership team utilizes Bomb Bomb to send video email invites to recruits during prospecting, and also video follow up emails. The receiver gets to see my face, and feel like they connect with me when I mention them by name in the video with a sincere "thank you Mike for taking the time with me today."

I have become a terribly busy guy over the years, and now running three companies, my time is stretched. So video email also allows a busy leader to leverage relationships through quick videos. Bomb Bomb has an app so that even if I am out and about, or in the airport, I can instantly send a video. I also love the video emails for personal recognition, which our employees and teams need on occasion. In "RE-Humanize" they share results from a survey that showed the top three issues employees have with their leaders. They were:

1. Not recognizing employee achievements (63%)

   As I've already mentioned, video provides a very personalized way for you to smile and send a private message to the recipient for a job well done. We also do the same publicly, when appropriate as well. Because video is so readily available, it allows me as a leader to let my people know that I do care about the job they do, and it shows in my video.

2. Not giving clear direction (57%)

   How many times as a leader have you been frustrated by a task not getting done correctly? I know I have several times as a leader. Most of the time I reread my emails (looking in the mirror first) and discovered the message could have been misinterpreted. Video allows for much more concise instruction.

3. Not having enough time to meet with employees. (53%)

   This is sometimes out of our control. Utilizing video to still see my employees and sales teams has been powerful. With Bomb Bomb it even allows them to respond via video so that you can see them back, and ensure they received the information, or kudos.

Also, let the truth come out that occasionally you don't wear make-up. That occasionally you wear t-shirts. That occasionally you make mistakes. It will allow you to make leaps and bounds in growing your relationships with your teams. There is a human element to not being perfect.

If you have not been convinced yet to add video as part of your leadership, then let me read one last passage from the Re-Humanize Your Business book. "You're going to communicate more clearly, build trust and rapport more quickly, differentiate yourself from competitors, and improve customer experience by being yourself."

I have been a customer with Bomb Bomb for almost 8-years and have sent over 1000 videos and the frequency has only increased in recent years. I will likely be at 2000 by the end of this year.

If you are not using video in your work, start now. With your customers and with your employees. Then watch the leader within you that gets uncovered by doing so.

CHAPTER 11

Leaders Reflect & Show Care

C an you sense from the last chapter that I LOVE VIDEO? And as time goes by, I will increase the frequency at which I record and share video across many different channels. However, I would be remiss if I did not share that nothing beats a personal hand-written note. Yes, a video allows the receiver to see you, and to see that you are human, and sincere in your message which builds trust over time. I have already mentioned how video allows you to leverage yourself because you can do several in a short period of time or even record one video that gets emailed to hundreds of people at once.

But a personal handwritten note takes time. As a result of the time it takes, the receiver is typically blown away by the gesture. So even though I send many more videos than I do handwritten notes, I must say that when I need a message to count, it is the handwritten note. If I need the message timely, I send a video.

I remember one time when I was in sales being taught myself the power of the handwritten note. I was invited for dinner at one of my best client's homes. Over the years I had sent him many personal notes. When he brought me into his office to show me something, I saw a stack of my personal notes (probably 3 years' worth) sitting on a side table next to some reading glasses. It was then that I truly ended up understanding the amazing power of a handwritten note. It's been told many times that the reason they are so powerful is because they take the most precious asset we are given in life. Time. And when you invest time in writing a note to a client, or an employee, they know it and many of them will keep it. When you yourself have received a personal handwritten note, how did it make you feel? Did you feel appreciated and more connected with the person who gave it to you? I would bet, yes!

I have kept almost all of the handwritten notes that I've received from my staff and salespeople over the years. And every time I get one, it brings a smile to my face. I value my relationship with that person at a higher level. If you are not writing personal notes as a daily practice, I would start immediately. As a leader, speak from your heart. I often found myself writing on four primary topics:

1. How are you and the family? (Shows that you care about their personal life)
2. Great job on that project, you are an asset to our company. (Recognition)
3. It was great chatting with you earlier today. (If you ran into them in the hallway, breakroom, or chatted briefly on the phone with them)
4. If I can be of any assistance, feel free to reach out. (Transparency and an open door)

Hardly anyone write notes anymore. Why is this? I've written 1000's over the years, and so has my wife Renee. Together it has been a pillar that has been part of building a foundational relationship with people. We did it when we sold real estate with our clients and vendors. We still write notes today as leaders to our staff, real estate agents, our loan officers in our mortgage company and folks we are trying to recruit into our company. We even make it a practice to send personal notes to guests on our podcast and Executives at our parent company. Gratitude is missing in this world, and a personal note can help show your grateful heart.

Even though the notes are embedded as part of our daily and weekly routines, they aren't just a check box type item but coming from a place of care. We are deliberate in who we write to. We truly seek out those who need their spirits lifted. Who did a great job on a project recently? Who had something tragic in their personal life happen? Your people will care about the company, and care about you as their leader only AFTER they feel that you genuinely care about them. We have all heard the saying, "People don't care how much you know, until they know how much you care."

I highly encourage you to make writing notes standard tactics for your other leaders in your organization as well. Writing notes shows the recipient care. Writing notes helps you retain folks who maybe did not think you cared at all about them, their family, or the job they do for you. When writing notes, be careful to not be selective who you write to. Show that you care about them all. Also, make it part of your daily routine. I currently write five personal notes a day. For you it might be less, or more. Depends on the size of your company or department. Keep a spreadsheet to ensure you are reaching out to everyone in your organization frequently throughout the year. Now, this number might change from month to month, but you should have consistent notes that you are writing.

Don't stop with staff, agents and vendors. What about competitors? What about trainers or corporate folks at your parent company? What about the people in Starbucks that make your coffee every day? Don't underestimate what this can do with the spirit of the receiver.

I remember my mentor Brian Buffini use to always say, "Nothing has been more powerful in my business, created more referrals over the years, and taken such little time and money, as a handwritten personal note." The moment you understand this truth as a leader, you will transform the relationships around you. For me, a note can be written in just a few minutes. No excuses. It is a timeless principle.

In the book "The Art of Thank You—Crafting Notes of Gratitude", they share many ways to enhance the impact on personal notes. They share that "Nothing can replace the acknowledgement of a kind deed better than a handwritten note from the heart."

I should also mention that there are companies that will send out note cards that look like they are handwritten, but they are not. Those don't take time and won't be received the same way. I strongly urge you to invest the time. The process of picking up a pen and putting pen to paper is transformative. I feel like you lay down the ink and the receiver picks it up on the other end. It's almost as if you are connected via ink. That is how relationships and connections are built stronger, not by taking the short cut.

A JOB WELL DONE

How do we know if we are being good leaders in our company? Or that we are respected as a leader at all? Do we get showered with gifts?

Being a leader in any industry is truly a thankless job. Especially if you are the owner or highest Executive within an organization. There may be no one above you to give some atta boys or atta girls.

Luckily, WE have found several of our people over the years express their gratitude in many ways. From writing a traditional thank you in a personal handwritten note, or maybe by offering to buy us lunch or coffee on occasion. Obviously, we do not wait for the thank you cards to do our job. But they are so appreciated when we receive them. I suggest saving some of the personal handwritten notes from your people. We all have rough days. But when you do, pull out those cards and re-read them. They will put a smile back on your face and inspire you to push through.

Our Mission / Vision / Values / Beliefs drive us every day to move the company forward. To do what's right for our staff and agents. Good leaders recognize that if we help enough agents get what they want, then we too will get what we want. Win / win.

Leaders will extend help when they see that their people need it. They do not wait for their people to ask for help. Instead, they provide the necessary help or tools when there is a need. As a leader, we must be looking for a need. I find myself offering help almost every time I speak with someone from my organization, even though I don't even feel that they need it. The thought process is that I am conveying that I am open to help SHOULD they ever need it. And that is invaluable to most folks.

I can't tell you how many times we have bought books for our agents when we heard a need. Or motivational signs with quotes to pump them up when they are feeling down. Or décor for their office suites that allows them to focus and be in a comfortable environment when working or prospecting. I can't tell you when the need will come. But you must keep an eye out for it. Most recently I had an agent I was coaching talk to me about major depression she was experiencing, and she was contemplating getting out of the business. She said, I'm not sure what I need to be doing in my life right now, but I am doubting my abilities as an agent. What I heard her say was that she was flailing. She did not know her true purpose in life, and that was causing major anxiety.

I asked her if she had ever read the book, "Start with Why" by Simon Sinek? She said "No!" So, I said, "Well, I have a copy in my office I am staring at. If I gave you the book, can you read it before our next coaching call next month?" She agreed to do so, and we are off and running. I wrote an incredibly positive message on the inside cover, to keep her positively focused on the outcome.

Keeping an eye out for a need. We have learned this idea years ago from Brian Buffini as well. Identify the need, then fill the need. When it comes to helping our people get just a little better today than yesterday, we need to focus them on taking the NEXT step. My coach Tyrone says "If they are laying down, get them to sit up. If they are sitting up, then get them to stand up. And if they are standing, get them to take that first step." Incremental changes in someone will pay dividends over the years. Meet your people where they are at. Help them take that NEXT step. Don't force someone laying down to jump up and start running. Leaders understand there is a progression and a patience needed to achieve great things.

Leaders create joy without being told to. Putting smiles on the faces of your people. That's how you know you are doing a good job as a leader. It's another way to tell the difference between a manager and being a leader.

JOURNALING AS A LEADER

I was first introduced to the idea of a journal years ago, in one of the success books I read. Then I saw the journaling idea pop up in other books as I read more, and then listened to great mentors discuss the power of journaling. I will tell you that it is not a habit that is easily formed. For me, I struggled with "What do I write?" "What do I say?" "What's the purpose?"

I plan to answer all of these as I tell you my journey to journaling. I will also share why it is a success trait that needs to be adapted if you aren't currently doing it consistently.

I have owned many journals in my life and been given several as gifts, maybe you have too. I have started writing in each of them, and somewhere I have a collection of journals that I made it through, roughly 10 entries in each before giving up.

I struggled greatly with what to put in the journal, which crippled me from being consistent as well.

It wasn't until I did Hal Elrod's 30-Day Challenge from his book "Miracle Morning", that I learned to be consistent. With the 30-Day Challenge, it literally is "Scribing" every day for thirty days. That's part of his S-A-V-E-R-S routine, but an important one.

And now, after years of starting and stopping. Buying several journals and wasting my money, I have found the perfect recipe for consistent success in journaling. Here it is:

— First, you need to know why journaling is beneficial. I've got three reasons why I believe journaling will change your life and help you become more successful in many faucets as a leader.

1. Similar to what I shared about writing handwritten personal notes, and putting "pen to paper," journaling has this same benefit. Except with a journal, it is meant for your eyes only (in most cases). There is something immensely powerful about picking up a pen and reflecting on what makes sense to write today. When you write into a book, it feels much more permanent, and you will find yourself connecting deep within your mind and putting those thoughts on paper. It is something exceedingly difficult to explain, but unlike typing on a document or on your computer, writing with pen, really opens the mind and allows a deeper form of thinking. Now that said, if writing in a journal truly is not your thing, then at a minimum type and record in a word document. Or download one of the many journaling apps that exist.

2. Reflection. Often we find ourselves wondering, "How did I get to where I am in life." Journaling allows you to record your life. I can go back a year ago and see what struggles, if any were affecting me or my business. Or, I can see if I had any personal struggles that maybe I've gotten through. Successes

recorded can be huge to reflect on when things look grim today. Reflection is a powerful thing for a leader. It allows you to remember that your journey is not easy. It reminds you what you did to overcome challenges. It allows you to talk about great employees and document why they are helping your business so as to repeat those same qualities in others you hire. I can go on, but it is just so incredibly powerful to document your life. Recording the truth of your life. Good or bad. In business and in your personal life.

3. Maintaining a positive mindset. My favorite reason for journaling is to keep me thinking and keep me sharp. Try to focus mostly on the positive things that happen throughout the day and try to rarely record negative thoughts. You do need to record challenges and how you are handling them, and whether your actions worked or not. With COVID-19, my wife and I have been journaling a bunch since it started affecting our business and life. We need this journaled so that if and when something of this scale comes into our life again, we can see how the world responded, we can see how our industry responded, and we can see how WE responded. All of this is important to be even more on point if there is another time of something so devastating to society. This will help us reflect next time we are faced with adversity. BUT, those will hopefully be rare in your journal. Positive accomplishments, no matter how small. That's what I record. And, any upcoming events, travel, vacation, etc that you are looking forward to. This keeps you moving forward as a leader with a smile on your face as opposed to dwelling on the negative things.

— You need a journal. Is there a trick for the size journal, the color of the journal? Does it matter if it's hard bound or leather? On this topic, there is no true clear answer that works for everyone.

For some, the free journals that sometimes are given to us from vendors or companies are good enough. For others like myself, I realized I would appreciate the idea of journaling more if I went and invested in a nice one that was leather bound with a design that was more fitting to my personality. My current journal was $50 and has a leather cover with drawstrings to close it. It also has a tree on it, which is a powerful element to ME. But they have journals that have Unicorns. That have success quotes. That have animals. If you think it will help by purchasing one YOU picked out, then go do that. Most larger book retailers have them, and smaller selections in stores like Target.

— Next you need to know what to write in your journal? This is a question I got asked so many times in my life when I suggest that you should journal. It took me personally years of trial and error to find the best things to journal to make it a habit so that you WANT to continue. As mentioned above in one of my top three reasons to journal, positive reflection will make you a better leader, so maybe start there. You might also utilize a journal that prompts you each day if you really struggle. A recent book that I write in alongside my personal journal is a book called "Positive Disruption" by Tony Rubleski. This book is amazing and offers this sort of prompting. In this book, Tony shares a thought-provoking quote, and then asks you a question. Then, he provides space for you to answer and record your thoughts for that day. There are 365 quotes and questions in the book, so everyday you can start building this journaling habit.

Have you ever had an incredibly busy and exhausting day and yet there is still WAY too much left to do? We feel like a failure. We have a hard time keeping a smile on our face because we are overwhelmed with our "to-do" list.

It took me years of practice, but I have determined that focusing on what you DID get done today and writing THAT into your journal will be huge for your progress. I think we often do think we didn't get much done, but if you focus on the things you did accomplish when reflecting on the day, you will be shocked at how much truly got done. This will allow you to give yourself a break instead of beating yourself up over what didn't get done.

If you struggle to find positives from the day to journal about, or maybe you had a rough day and didn't get much done, then maybe journal something you are grateful for. No matter how small. For example, do you have means to have a meal today? Journal that you are grateful that you live in a place with healthy food options that you can afford. There are so many people living on the streets and they may not know where their next meal is coming from. We have so much to be grateful for and writing these into a journal is transformative.

What about focusing on a different employee in your organization each day. What are some great things about that person? Maybe there are things they do that make you smile. Maybe they are snazzy at how they dress. Maybe they are very attentive to the company's needs? They show up to work on time and are always willing to stay if needed? They are amazing at motivating others in the company. So many good qualities in our people. Find them and make that your journal entry. It will open a deeper appreciation for your people, which will lead to sending out thank you notes to those same employees over the years.

Back to the book "The Art of Thank You", they mention how sending a handwritten note is warmer and more powerful than just an email. If journaling does inspire you to write some notes to staff, try and ink those out, versus type them and email.

See how that worked? Journaling will open your mind to really deepen and strengthen relationships with your employees. First by thinking about the positives they bring to your company, and then by writing that handwritten note to them, thanking them for being a contributor to your organization.

If you are still thinking, Scott, I just can't still seem to figure out what to write in this journal. How about this? Think of one thing or person you are grateful for in life and just write that. "I am grateful for my wife." It can be that simple. "I am grateful for my house." I am grateful for "Football." (was that just me? Lol). Truly the hardest thing with journaling is just building the habit of doing it. So even writing today's date, and one word, will build that habit. 7/12/2020 "Grateful." Done. Next day, 7/13/2020 "Alive." You get the point.

Leaders will not deny this fact and will appreciate that grateful things can and should be journaled.

— How often should you journal? As I mentioned, I highly encourage you to make it a daily habit. Have you ever heard that "Consistency is Key?" In so many areas of life, but certainly as it pertains to journaling. I am currently living a structured morning routine which involves me journaling after I read every morning. My morning routine is about an hour and half long, and the journaling part of it is about 10 minutes and always immediately after reading. I find that often by doing it after reading that my mind is fresh with great stuff from the book. I am ready to start putting pen to paper. I even sometimes make journal entries as I read. Great passages from the books I read end up in my journal. Or, I sometimes journal action steps based on something I am currently reading. I typically journal about ½ page to a full page each day. BUT...I have journal entries that are one sentence, and I have other days where I ramble on for three pages or more. Because I have gotten into this routine of daily journaling, in the morning, I just don't feel right on the days I miss, which are very far and few between.

My journal entry each morning is a two part: What went great yesterday and what did I accomplish? And then what am I looking forward to today? I don't dwell on what didn't get done. I don't discuss the crappy things that happened yesterday and the major fires I had to put out.

And THAT, is how you can help your journey to being a great leader. By utilizing your journal as a way of maintaining a positive attitude daily. You'll that things really have to go sideways throughout the day in order to get into a negative mindset. And your positive attitude each day, in front of your people, translates into more smiles around the office, and more work getting done overall. Keep in mind, that YOU are responsible for the overall morale of your company or work environment.

— Last tip, encourage others around you to journal. For the same reasons I gave above, share this with them. In fact, if you have it in the budget and really want to show them you care about their mental state and helping to keep them positive thinking, then buy your team journals. We teach a yearlong class called "ELITE Group," and discuss the power of journaling often in this class, but rarely do we find that they are consistent with journaling. So we decided to put a quote on a journal and get them custom, company journals. Some nice leather ones. They LOVE it, and many of them, like me, now journal each day.

The quote we put on those journals was, "Good things come to those who HUSTLE." But I would change it now to "Good things come to those who journal positivity."

CHAPTER 12

Leaders Give

Do you give? I mean truly give with no expectation of return. No quid pro quo? It has been my experience that the companies that tend to do better in the long run and have more consistent long-lasting success, are companies that have a culture of giving back. And for a company to have this culture, it requires a leader who emulates this within their organization and incorporates it into their Mission / Vision or Core Values. "Community Driven" is a Core Value at our companies. As part of our description for that Core Value we mention that without our community, we would not be in business. Think about this in two different ways.

First: If you are a sales organization, like Real Estate, car sales, Insurance, Mortgage Lending, Financial Advisor and others, then you rely on your community to get sales and do make money. If you are a retail shop owner or restaurant owner, then you rely on the community to frequent your establishment or you will be out of business.

Second: If you have ANY employees that work physically in your company, then they live in the communities that surround your company. Their kids go to school in the schools around your office, warehouse, or shop. They are representatives of YOU and your company when they are out and about mingling with other community members.

As you can see, your business relies firsthand on the community shopping with you directly or using your services. Your staff and employees rely on the community for their kids schooling, their own shopping, and their own wellbeing. Community is extremely important. And so, giving back and being active in the community is important.

In my first example, people like to use the services of and frequent places where they feel like the person is not just about sales. They are not greedy. They are contributors themselves to making the community a better place.

In my second example, your ability to retain can be impacted. There is a cost a company incurs when it comes to training and rehiring. Ensure you are doing your part to limit your turnover, hence future rehiring costs. Be involved in things locally that are important to your people. Support their kids Little League baseball team. Sponsor a local non-profit event. Rally your employees to do a 5k to help raise money for local charities.

We have specific non-profits that we support every year. Big Brothers' Big Sisters, Children's Miracle Network, Local Food Banks, Christmas House, to name a few. BUT we want to know of and support other charities that are important to our staff as well. What we have found is that even in times of crisis, when money is plentiful to our people, they give. In fact, we have seen even higher amounts of giving during times of challenge. It is crazy what I have witnessed in our own organization and the amount of giving. It needs to be a focus of the company and leadership, and it needs to come from the heart.

Ask yourself, "What am I passionate about?" Start there. Dedicate yourself, or someone in your company to be the point person for ensuring you are meeting the needs of the community. Don't know where to start? Post on social media. ISO: Nonprofits that need volunteers or fundraising.

There are several ways to show your support and to give. Let me identify three main categories.

1. Money. Probably the most obvious way to give is financially. With our organization, real estate agents can give out of each home sale to Children's Miracle Network. Over the course of the year, this amounted to over $45k consistently year after year. One small donation, compounded with several more donations from others, turns into a big donation by the year's end. I know several companies that do this same type of giving out of an employee's paycheck. For example, $20 each pay period goes to United Way, or the Red Cross, or whatever. Those small donations add up. Don't discount them.

   Also, there are always great sponsorship opportunities that might make sense for you as well. Sponsorships are a good way to give to a needed charity, while getting your name out in front of the community. It is a by-product of sponsoring. But, if a parent of a little league baseball player knew you sponsored their kid's team, then who do you think they will remember that next time they need to order pizza (if you own a pizza place), or need to buy or sell real estate (if you are in real estate)? It's just how it works. You give and sponsor because it's our community. And in time, the community will remember that and support you too.

2. Volunteer to work for a cause. I can't begin to tell you how many times we have "rallied the troops" to go volunteer. Whether it be for a park clean up, working at a toy drive at Christmas, or volunteering to collect food for the needy. Non-profits rely heavily on volunteers, and good leaders will find ways throughout the year, to help fill those needs from the local charities.

3. Become a Board member of a non-profit. I love being a board member and have had the opportunity to serve on several boards over the years. I have been Chairman of the Board in the past for other non-profits, and currently sit on one nonprofit board for Seattle Children's Leadership Council and also Chair a Non-Profit that we founded called "Making Miracles Support Foundation." It is such a humbling experience and yet there's not much required to being a board member. You have a time commitment, of typically attending their monthly board meetings, but it puts you and your company in front of other business professionals that are on the board with you. If you need anything, these folks are typically first to step up and give. I love being on non-profit boards. There is no pay, it is voluntary. In addition, they typically ask for a contribution each year from you or your company to be on the board. As a result of my time on various boards, I have been able to get additional volunteering and fundraising done by others in my company because they want to support what's important to me and the company. And therefore, I always am open to helping with their needs for charity in the community as well.

If your company does not currently have an intentional budget for giving or sponsoring non-profit events, then I highly recommend getting this idea into the budget. It shows up on our annual budget for all the companies we own. It is one of my favorite lines. To me, an organization cannot have a complete budget, without this "expense" category.

We breed a culture where anyone one of our folks feels safe to ask us if we can rally the troops to go run a 5k for Parkinson's, or Bowl for Big Brothers Big Sisters. Or attend an auction for Children's Miracle Network. All of these we have done and then some.

The question then becomes, what is the need in your community? What are your people already doing that you can further their cause and expand their reach? Remember, your company cannot work without the community and the people in it. It is up to us as leaders to understand this truth, and do our part to make a difference in the communities that we are working in. Managers sometimes struggle to grasp this concept but moving from a manager to a leader requires a deeper desire to move employees, to move communities and to move the company forward.

This is achievable due to caring. Invest in your people and communities and you will see a return on that investment.

CHAPTER 13

Leading with FUN

I remember the day as if it were yesterday when I spent eight straight hours going through word choice for what would eventually be my Mission Statement, Vision Statement, and the CORE Values for my company. I realized quick that so many companies have words like "Honorable", or "Trustworthy", or "Honesty & Integrity" as their CORE values.

The gentleman that was helping me craft my company Mission Statement, Vision and CORE Values was saying that you don't want to be like everyone else. Steve, was his name. He was incredibly wise and a master at crafting a perfect MVVB.

After really diving deep within my mind and pulling out of me very unique word choices and core values that aren't typical, we ended up with CORE Values of Collaboration, Consistency, Character, Personal Growth, Community Driven, Focused and Fun.

I want to focus on FUN in this chapter. To have an engaged staff and engaged company where everyone gives a darn, then fun needs to be incorporated. If you are in sales of any kind, you likely have had your moment of being beat up and spit out. Many of us, including myself have dealt with neighbors using another real estate agent, besides the agent living right next to them. We have dealt with our closest friends and relatives NOT using us to sell their home. Or, USING us for information, and then going a different direction. It is a tough business, and I had to learn to take the good with the bad.

When sitting in a conference room in 2014 with Steve, going through what would eventually be my MVVB, I decided that "FUN" needed to be incorporated as a CORE Value. In today's crazy tech savvy world, there are many companies putting foosball and pool tables into their offices as if that would create an amazing culture and atmosphere that would attract others. WRONG! It CAN help bring a sense of community within an organization, but a great culture is not built off a game or an espresso machine in the break room.

As you build your team, or office, incorporate FUN into the workplace. Finding ways to make it fun will be a crucial aspect of the team or office succeeding.

We need to make light of the fact that sometimes we have lows in our individual businesses. There also can be amazing highs. Whether there are highs or lows, we need to make sure we are having fun along the way. For us, we had several ways that we did this. I LOVE contests. So first and for most, consider contests.

For an office, I would say that telling your staff that you will give prizes for folks that attend meetings, or that you will do a drawing for attendance of key trainings, etc., will result in excitement and also loyalty of them wanting to attend. Not only might they win something, but they will learn something amazing, while having fun. Many company owners, and department leaders only care about how much money they can make, and not finding ways to make sure their people are enjoying the ride along the way.

As a team leader of a high producing Top 1% real estate team back in my day, I would create a threshold that if we hit it as a team, then there would be a reward. I got this idea from Joe Niego, an amazing brokerage owner and Top producer from Chicago. He used to have a challenge to hit so many transactions for himself in peak months like May.

I decided to incorporate this same concept. I think our goal one year was to do 15 home sales in the month of May. If we hit it, then everyone would get to go on an all-expense paid trip, like weekend getaway type thing. Nothing that would break the bank, but something that got all our team on board with hitting it hard with prospecting in the months leading up to May. We never had a problem hitting those numbers. This can be incorporated into any business or industry.

Who doesn't like a good competition? I remember when I was at Starbucks as a General Manager. There was a push back in 2000 to sell Espresso machines. Starbucks is not really in the espresso machine business anymore, but in 2000 they were still a young company, growing fast and trying to find their way. This contest caused me as a General Manager to think outside the box. The prize was something like $4000 Bonus to the Manager that won. I decided to tell my staff that the bonus would be split amongst all of them if we won. Together we created an amazing plan and marketing scheme that won us the contest that year. In fact, we ended up having the highest sales in one day than any other Starbucks store at the time in the entire network. FUN. That is what's important. We all were kids once. We all don't like stress. How do we incorporate FUN into our businesses? For me, it starts by making it a CORE Value, and making sure you do things throughout the year that show your staff that it is an important CORE Value.

We also do an annual bus trip to Leavenworth., WA. Leavenworth is a fun, German themed town in Central Washington. It is one of the most fun things we do. We also have fun at our holiday parties by incorporating FUN into the party, like Ugly Sweater contests and more.

Be creative in however you do it. Remember that just putting a foosball table or pool table into your office, does not make you cool. It does not automatically add "FUN" to your company.

I have also seen creative themed holiday parties, BBQ areas added to offices to enjoy a relaxing lunch mid-week, fun giveaways to your sales reps and employees. Think outside the box on this, but the main point is that if you want to create a culture that is attractive and that people want to stay at, add an element or two of FUN. If you are not the creative one in your organization, then make sure someone on your staff is responsible for helping with this. Maybe hire a Director of Fun?

CHAPTER 14

Leaders Create Value

M any leaders do not end up succeeding. Most businesses are lucky to make it 4-5 years before they go out of business. Some don't make it a year or two. Why is this?

The successful leaders tend to know their value, and how to show it to their clients. It all starts with creating a great Mission Statement, Vision Statement and Core Values. If you don't know what you stand for, or don't fully know where you should be going, then success will become much more challenging. Then you just need to make sure that you understand what makes you different.

Putting this in real estate terms, it's like an agent that goes on an appointment where she may be competing for the listing against several other Realtors. That agent needs to first show the sellers why she is unique and what she does different than the others. After they are selected, the topic of commission rate comes up. Successful listing agents tend to clearly know their value. What makes them stand out. And if the seller asks them to lower their commission, they are typically prepared to reshare that value proposition and why they are worth what the fees will be.

Same thing applies in any business. What makes your item more appealing than your competitors? Why do you charge what you charge? What truly separates you from your competition? Do you know? Can you explain it?

Managers typically are good at selling the value of what they do. Leaders are the ones that create it. See the difference? It's up to the leader to help create the atmosphere, the morale of the staff, the quality of the product, etc.

So is being a leader all about creating? In a way, yes. It is about building something that can be managed. People, services, and products can be managed. But experiences, atmosphere and culture is built by leaders who dream a bit. They put into motion the specific blueprint that a manager can then go run with. Is it possible to have a company with no managers and only leaders? Absolutely. I believe it's the best of both worlds. To have great leadership at high levels, and lower-level leaders that follow the examples you have laid out. The processes you have created.

We have heard it said many times, that cost is only an issue in the absence of value. Try your best to provide exceptional value. Meaningful value to your customer or clients. I say this, because I think sometimes we can think that the COST of a resource equals value. It does not. For example, in my market print advertising has just not provided the value to the real estate agent that it once did. And even though the cost of print advertising, which is not the lowest, can be perceived as high value, it just does not have the return anymore. As mentioned previously, I would do a survey or poll to determine what agents really are looking for. If for example you knew you were getting ready to invest in a resource for that costs $1000 a month, then polling the people that are going to benefit from this new resource or tool would be valuable.

Maybe ask your clients what they prefer? They can help you choose different levels of service, or different products based on their feedback. The things they will share can help retain them as customers, and likely will be the things that will attract a new clientele as well.

Here are just a few examples of things that can create value:

- Location of your store or office
- Price of your service or product
- Quality of your product
- Exceptional communication
- Fast response time
- Multiple locations
- Exceptionally training or highly skilled staff
- Special order capabilities
- Options for various sizes and colors or different products

Good leaders, in any industry know what separates them from their competition. And because technology is advancing so quickly it becomes even more important to really understand what separates you from the rest.

Let's do an exercise now to see if we can get you started if you don't quite know in your own company. Make a list below of all the things that YOU provide in your office or store that adds value to your clients.

1. _____
2. _____
3. _____
4. _____
5. _____
6. _____
7. _____
8. _____
9. _____
10. _____

Did you find 10 things? If not, you need more to really show true value.

Next, look at this list again and ask yourself, am I the ONLY one, or one of the only ones that provides THAT specific thing to the consumer? In other words, if you put down that you open at 5AM (early for your industry) then is that really something only you do? Maybe not.

Put a star next to any item you honestly believe is something maybe only you or possibly only one other company in your market does.

These star items are what separates you. They are the true value propositions that you need to ensure you share consistently with your current clients.

If you only had one or two, or maybe even only three starred items, then likely you need to work on adding more value to your company. You may say, "But Scott it costs money to add more value." True. Cost is only an issue in the absence of value, remember? If you don't want to find ways to add more value to your company, then consider this when you set the cost of your products or service. Otherwise, you will never attract enough customers to become profitable or stay profitable.

If you are looking for more value to add but don't know where to start, go back to your existing clients or even your staff. Ask them, "what are we missing here at this company that you wish we had?" If you sell a product, maybe ask, "How else can we make this product easier to use, or more user friendly?" Ask you staff what they have heard customers complain about. Don't underestimate the power of surveys. Again, it is why so many companies add survey links to receipts these days. You can only get better, if you know what areas need improving.

In 2010, Dominos Pizza changed a few things pertaining to their pizzas based on customer feedback. They also realized that their customers were itching for an easier way to order pizza and so they took a deep dive towards digital. That shift caused them to make the statement, "We used to be a pizza company that sells online, and now we are an e-commerce business that sells pizza."

CONCLUSION

I'm ready to become a leader.
Now what?

My wife and I have learned through over a decade of ownership and amazing growth over the years, that if you take care of your people, they will ultimately take care of you. There is an old Zig Ziglar quote that goes, "You will have all you want in life, if you help enough other people get what they want."

This is an idea that should be embraced. In real estate, we don't look at it as: If we add more agents then I can make more money. But rather, when I help my agents increase their business, sell more homes, and achieve their life aspirations...then the money will be there.

So as you start to think about what few nuggets you got out of this book, I want you to remember that if you lead from the heart, find new ways to give, then you will be profitable and attract the right people to your company and culture.

Don't let this be just another book that you read and put back on the shelf. What one or two ideas are you going to act on? Not next year, not in two years, NOW! Maybe you buy and read the book

"Re-Humanize"? Maybe you buy a journal and start to build that daily habit? Maybe you buy some personal notes and commit to a goal to write "X" number each day or each week. Maybe for you it's creating a Mission / Vision / Core Values for your company or for your department?

Now is the time to improve as a leader. Now is the time to implement. And now is the time to make a mark in your industry.

Thank you for investing time in yourself and in this book. Until the next one...

A WORD ON TRAINING

For Leaders That Train or Oversee a Training Department

Proper training of employees on the front end is crucial in shaping the foundation for a great workforce. Great leaders understand the value in investing proper time into training someone. As frustrating as it sometimes is to have to invest this time, the level of production that will come from the individual is so much greater. Versus the manager that just throws these folks onto the frontlines, hoping they know what to do or abdicating the duties.

This can lead to poor performance, poor customer service, and eventually churn of the employee. Not to mention, the stress of hiring a replacement.

ELIMINATING TURNOVER

Once I worked for a large Coffee Retailer who assigned me to take over one of their flagship stores in San Jose, CA. This store had not been profitable in many years. They brought me in to see if I can find the issue. And I did. After analyzing the profit & loss statements, I saw that the "TRAINING" line item was drastically higher than in other stores and certainly higher than budgeted. I asked the current store manager why this was? She stated it was because they constantly turn people over. They just cannot get staff to stay long and they always seem to be hiring. This is a problem, a big problem. Payroll tends to a be a company's top expense, and if constant hiring and retraining is a huge part of this, it will eventually put a company out of business. This is not to say training is not important. Proper training is crucial to the future success of an organization. The companies that know this and create training plans for their new hires, become extraordinarily successful and limit turn over.

To limit turnover, one of the top things you can do is look at the culture of the company. Also, their training. Lastly, being able to deliver constructive feedback timely and rewarding good behavior or results, will lead to lower turnover. This is absolutely a time where I will say, if you have a turnover problem at your company, look in the mirror. It all starts with the leader. If they do not directly report to you, then you need to change or adjust what you have your lower-level leaders doing with the staff. It typically comes down to having consistent systems that all leaders abide by.

I remember once being asked to speak at an International Conference on the topic of Recruiting. Those sessions always had lots of people because recruiting is hard to do and keeping a sharp mind on new ideas is key. I thought about why we had success with recruiting over the years and it comes down to us having a solid culture that is easy to recruit to. As in my turnover example above, if you have things broken in your company, it doesn't matter how many people you hire and bring on, they will eventually leave. They will get frustrated and quit.

Before you think about adding a staff person, create a perfect job description and a detailed training plan as to what the training is on day 1. Also, who is going to be training them? Day 2, what is the focus, and who's training them?

If you have good systems for training and the rest of your company has a good culture that is positive, productive, and collaborative, then you are ready to hire and have a thriving business. Always look in the mirror. If you have a turnover problem then YOU are the common denominator, right?

CLASSROOM SETTING

Often, we find ourselves in a classroom setting with employees. So how do we improve the results that we expect out of the classroom environment?

An article published by Edutopia.com stated, "Effective classroom management requires awareness, patience, good timing, boundaries, and instinct. There's nothing easy about shepherding a large group of easily distractible people with different skills and temperaments along a meaningful learning journey." Do you think the real estate agents in my company are highly distractible? Absolutely they are. Even when in a classroom, they are hoping their phone rings because it MIGHT be a new client. They will walk out of the classroom in the middle of the instructor talking to grab an "unknown caller" with the hopes it is a new client.

Before I share with you some of my tips for getting results from a classroom, I think it is important for you to get context as to what my teaching experience is. I have spoken all over the country and trained over 100 classroom sessions with an audience anywhere from 2 people up to almost a thousand. I have taught other people's content, but also, I have created custom content and unique classes that drive results.

That said, let me give you my tips on how to get results from the classes and trainings you do. Some of what I will share does go along with what Edutopia.com stated in their article.

BOUNDARIES

I am very firm on timeliness and on not cancelling a class once they have signed up. This may seem very elementary to most, but starting a class on time, and ending on time will garner great respect from those that attend. In my case, I mostly taught independent contractors who were not employees of mine. In other words, it could be conceived that setting boundaries would be more difficult to do when you are not technically their boss. Also, in this industry, a real estate agent can leave your company and go work for someone else in a heartbeat and for any stupid reason they want. And they sometimes do. That said, I would start my meetings on time and end on time ALWAYS. These professionals want to know that you have boundaries. If you start the class on time, how embarrassing is it for them to enter the classroom a couple minutes past the start time? In my case, VERY embarrassing. I do not ignore someone who walks into a room late. I acknowledge them in every case and point out that they are late, usually in a joking way. I never looked at this small tactic as cruel but rather as a teachable moment. The students would prefer to not get singled out, and so in time, if they knew I was teaching then they wanted to make sure they arrived on time.

I also eventually got to the point where we tied a core value at our company, Community Driven, with a penalty for being late. The policy was that a person would be required to donate $25 to Children's Miracle Network hospitals if they showed up late. If someone entered a few minutes late and I had already started the class I would say, "Thank you for the $25 donation. Don't feel bad though, it's for the kids." And

I would smile. Usually the other agents in the training would chuckle as well, which I assume made it a bit more awkward for the student.

What does this do in the heat of the moment? Probably upsets the person. What does it do for their memory for the next class they attend? Makes sure that they arrive on time. By the way, the rest of the class feels thankful that you started on time and showed that there is a consequence for the person that shows up late and disturbs the class. It also shows them that you respect THEIR time. By starting on time, and ending on time, this is what they are getting by your actions. You respect their time. I should point out that on occasion the classes did run long. I try extremely hard to stay on track and check the clock frequently throughout the training. But sometimes there are just longer dialogues or more questions, that leads to the class running behind. In these circumstances I always point out that the end time of the class has arrived, so if anyone needs to leave feel free. Otherwise, we are likely about 10 minutes away from wrapping up. This also shows the class that you are respecting their time. And in these circumstances, I do not give anyone a hard time for leaving at the original class end time.

The second half of this is the person who does not end up showing up to class after registering or RSVPing to attend. Why should we care about this? It is very disrespectful to the coordinator of the training or the instructor. Think about it, likely there were materials printed and lunch provided for that student only for them not to attend because they maybe had something more important pop up or more exciting.

I also had a consequence for this example as well. In my business we would send out monthly invoices for ala-carte items that a real estate agent would purchase from our brokerage. Well, if you miss a class that you registered for, then we add a $25 donation to Children's Miracle Network to the statement. Same penalty as if they were late. You get the point.

Think about your business and how you can incorporate this concept into your training. What can a potential penalty be?

It is also especially important to make sure that at the start of the class you set the expectations for the class and share an agenda. As you have probably heard many times, conflict only arises when expectations differ. I became particularly good at setting expectations with the attendees of the class. To help the class stay on track and on topic it's also good to get some buy in from the students as to what their expectations are for the session.

Some of the expectations were: Please silence your cell phone and do your best to avoid looking at your phone while in class; please do your best to use the restroom and return phone calls on the break. Give them an idea of when that break will come. This will prevent someone leaving while you are talking or teaching, which can be a distraction not only to you but also other students. If someone does walk out answering a call, I typically do chat with them on a break and ask that they try hard to not focus on their phone while in class. Especially since the breaks come roughly an hour to one and a half hours into the training. There aren't too many emergencies that happen where if you called back an hour later you couldn't handle it then. These principles also apply when training via ZOOM or other webinars.

Also, an expectation needs to be set about when you want them to ask questions as there most certainly will be some. In other words, do you prefer they hold their questions until the end? Until you have gotten through all the material? Or, do you prefer they just ask the questions as they come up? I have found I prefer they ask the questions as they think of them. They seem to be easier to answer if you can reference where you are in the program or class content.

PATIENCE – Have some but do not worry if it is only some.

It is most certainly a virtue, isn't it? In a classroom environment I have found myself many times answering the same question multiple times.

There were several times where I felt like folks were not listening or maybe they were playing on their phones while I explained something and now here they are asking. I had no problem saying, "As I explained already…." You must be truthful and not pretend that you did not cover the content. Be honest with yourself and let the other students in the class know that you noticed they are asking a question that was already addressed.

You may be thinking that I am a hard instructor. And I will say to a certain degree I am. I have little patience for folks that do not respect the classroom, especially after I set clear expectations up front. At the end of the day, I want the students to respect the instructor and the other students. We should not really care if they "like" the instructor, so long as they respect them.

That said, it is important to have a level of patience. Some content can be hard to grasp or understand so realize that sometimes we may need to re-explain something a different way to the same folks. Also understand that there may be more conversations within the classroom about the topic than you had anticipated. In these circumstances, be understanding and do your best to be patient with any frustration on the part of the student.

There also may be a student that is testing your patience throughout the class. How would you handle this situation? Again, I will go to a part of the article by Edutopia.com.

"I have never met a student that doesn't want to be successful. If they are misbehaving it is kind of like when a baby cries; there is something wrong in their world. If they are misbehaving for attention, then find out why they need the attention and how you can give them what they need."

When I experience these folks, I do address them often in the class, and ask them to answer many of the questions that need answering as the class goes on. I find that by engaging the disruptors, they learn more and it seems to change their tone as the class goes on.

In wrapping up this chapter I will say that I LOVE teaching in a classroom environment. I have really improved my skills to be at an exceptional level. That said, classroom environment training is what inspired me into writing this book. So often I taught amazing content. Content that if implemented would change the student's life forever. Yet so few took the ideas they learned and put them into practice. An even smaller sampling of students stayed consistent with what they learned. You would think that this would frustrate me to a level that would cause me to write this book, right? You can lead a horse to water, but you cannot make them drink it.

However, the real motivation to write this book came by watching the one student or maybe two in each class that took the content, implemented it and went on to have massive success. The agents in my company that literally took what they learned, by the teaching of those that lived before them, and then repeated it in their own businesses went on to become millionaires. Yes millionaires! THAT is what frustrated me. Trying to understand what causes THOSE folks to take action and watching our teachings do what we said they would, and then watching several others…a majority in fact, NOT do it. Then come to me later and complain. Why am I not having more success? I took the class they say. THIS was my motivation.

You might be asking how I responded to these statements from the underperforming?

Easy, I would tell the truth. That is what leaders do. Want to be a high performing leader? When your employees ask you tough questions you tell them what they need to hear, the truth.

"I taught you what to do to achieve your life aspirations, and you didn't do it. Want to achieve your goals and dreams? You must execute what you learned in the classroom, in the books you read, and from those that have lived before you."

ACKNOWLEDGEMENT

There are countless individuals that have helped pave the path to who I have become as a leader. Many have already been mentioned in this book. In addition, I wish to thank the following individuals that have contributed either knowingly or otherwise.

Renee Comey, COO / Co-Owner RE/MAX Elite and Motto Mortgage Elite and my wonderful wife

Lynette Gamm, Branch Leader for RE/MAX Elite and Top Producing Team Leader in Real Estate

Tyrone Davids, Scott's personal coach & CEO of EDI Performance in Toronto, Ontario Canada

Eric Penz, VP of Private Advisory Financial Management Group in Redmond, WA

DeDe Heggem, Top Producing Real Estate agent with RE/MAX Elite in Snohomish, WA

Mandy Fulford, CEO RE/MAX Southern Shores in Myrtle Beach, SC

Afrose Amlani, Owner & Head of School for Living Montessori in Bellevue, WA

ABOUT THE AUTHOR

Scott Comey is CEO of Motto Mortgage Elite and RE/MAX Elite. In addition, Scott and his wife own a coaching company called Turn the Dial Coaching, which incorporates a podcast to help business owners and real estate agents achieve great things.

Scott also founded a 501c3 non-profit called Making Miracles Support Foundation which raises funds and contributes to local children's hospitals. Scott holds a US Patent and has another Patent pending. Scott is immensely proud to sit on the Seattle Children's Leadership Council, and is a former Chairman of the Board for Big Brothers Big Sisters of Snohomish County.

He has been featured multiple times in Real Estate magazine by RisMedia, has been a regular contributor to news media regarding real estate in the Seattle market, and been a speaker at dozens of events in front of thousands of people across the country.

He and his wife have been coached themselves for many years, and they believe reading, journaling, coaching, and constant personal development are keys to success in anything you do.

CPSIA information can be obtained
at www.ICGtesting.com
Printed in the USA
FSHW020404270421